Songs and M
City of London

By Paul D Jagger and Julian Cable

First Edition published 2021

Printed by Short Run Press Limited, Exeter

This book is also available in eBook format from Amazon, Apple and Payhip.

This publication is dedicated to the memory of:

Alderman Sir Roger Gifford KStJ, 1955-2021

Lord Mayor of London, 2012-2013

Master of the Worshipful Company of Musicians, 2016-2017

Co-founder of City Music Foundation

A tireless advocate for music and the arts in the City of London

Contents

Acknowledgements

This guide would not have been possible without the support and contribution of many who have assisted in its development, review and publication.

The authors would like to recognise in particular the following individuals and institutions, whose time and inputs, gladly given, have been of substantial value. The authors apologise for any unintentional omissions from this list.

Sir Andrew Parmley, Lord Mayor (2016–2017), for the Foreword

Paul Campion, Leslie East, Michael Lewin, and Andrew Morris – Pastmasters, Worshipful Company of Musicians; and Hugh Lloyd, Clerk

William Alden, Clerk, Worshipful Company of Stationers and Newspaper Makers

Piers Baker, Clerk, Worshipful Company of Tin Plate Workers alias Wire Workers

David Barrett, Secretary, Fellowship of Clerks

Peter Bateman, Clerk, Armourers' Hall

Charlotte Borger, the Charterhouse

Mark Butler, Clerk, Worshipful Company of Glovers

Karen Cardy, Fiona Dinsdale and Tim Oldershaw, London Symphony Orchestra

Jeremy Cartwright, Denis Cruse and Jonathan Mead, Worshipful Company of Horners

Christine Cook, Guild of Freemen of the City of London

Ronald Corp, Liveryman, Worshipful Company of Musicians

Duncan Crole, Clerk, Worshipful Company of Woolmen

Gillian Croxford, Penelope Fussell and Richard Winstanley, Worshipful Company of Drapers

Anne Curry, Worshipful Company of Fletchers

Gaye Duffy and Mary Hardy, Worshipful Company of World Traders

The late Catherine Ennis, Director of Music, St Lawrence Jewry

Niki Gorick, Niki Gorick Photography Ltd

Penny Graham, Clerk, Worshipful Company of Cordwainers

The Reverend Robin Griffith-Jones, Guy Beringer, Carol Butler and Claire Hargrove, Temple Church and Temple Music Foundation

Ray and Irene Hall and Clive Tulloch

Joe Hardy, LSO St Luke's Marketing Co-ordinator, and Matthew Weinreb, photographer

Adrienne Harper, Clerk, Worshipful Company of Security Professionals

Stephen Henderson, Clerk, Worshipful Company of Tax Advisers

Mark Holford and Susan Hoefling, Worshipful Company of Information Technologists

Jo Hutchinson, Guildhall School of Music and Drama

The Very Reverend Dr David Ison, Dean of St Paul's Cathedral, and Pauline Stobbs, Communications Manager

Christian Jensen, Clerk, Worshipful Company of Educators

Colour Sergeant Anthony Johncock, Honourable Artillery Company

Matthew Johnson, Clerk, Worshipful Company of Environmental Cleaners

Richard Jones, Music Librarian, Barbican Music Library

The Reverend Canon Dr Alison Joyce, Rector, St Bride's Church

John Kelly, Barbican Centre

Cheyney Kent, The City Bach Collective

Julian Litchfield and Walter Gill, Worshipful Company of Carmen

Jonathan Louth, Worshipful Company of Chartered Architects

Phillip Ludgrove, Worshipful Company of Skinners

William Lyons, The City Musick

Edward Macey-Dare, Clerk, Worshipful Company of Distillers

Alastair MacQueen, Worshipful Company of Joiners and Ceilers

Shaun Mackaness, Clerk, Worshipful Company of Framework Knitters

Tessa Marchington, Managing Director, Music in Offices

Lt Col Tony Marinos, Clerk, Worshipful Company of Bowyers

Simon Meyer, Ancient Society of College Youths

Lisa Miller, Worshipful Company of Grocers

Oliver Nesbitt, Nick Bodger and Johanna Taylor, City of London Corporation

Michael O'Dwyer, Clerk, Worshipful Company of Brewers

Helen Ogilvie, Professional Proofreading

Lewis Phillips, Chairman, Lloyd's Choir

Kate Pink, Clerk, Worshipful Company of Fletchers

Stephen Plumb, Past Master of the Parish Clerks' Company, and Alana Coombes, Clerk

Jonathan Rennert, Director of Music, St Michael Cornhill

John Reynolds, Editor, City Events

Alex Robertson and Melissa Scott, Worshipful Company of Turners

Jenny Robinson, General Manager, City of London Choir and Director, Summer Music in City Churches

Nick Royle, Clerk, Worshipful Company of Apothecaries

Dr Michel Saminaden, Master, Worshipful Company of Tylers and Bricklayers

Richard Scott, Chairman and Company Secretary, The City of London Phonograph and Gramophone Society

Fiona Sedgwick, Clerk, Worshipful Company of Needlemakers

Fay Sonkin, Spitalfields Music

Kate Swan, London City Voices

Clare Taylor (Lady Gifford), City Music Foundation

Tony Tucker, The Friends of the City Churches

Katherine Walker, Worshipful Company of Salters

The Reverend Marcus Walker, Rector, The Priory Church of St Bartholomew the Great

Chris Wardle, Director of External Relations, VOCES8 Foundation

Neville Watson, Misha Hebel and Richard Townend, Worshipful Company of Scientific Instrument Makers

Tim Yap, Members' Manager, London City Orchestra

Foreword

After the great success of Paul Jagger's *The City of London Freeman's Guide*, it is wonderful to see him team up with Julian Cable, a Liveryman of our own Worshipful Company of Musicians, to produce *Songs and Music of the City of London.*

Not only is London the cultural capital of the world but its offer continues to grow under the careful stewardship of the City of London Corporation, the local authority for the Square Mile and the oldest continuous municipal authority in the world. Indeed, the City's plans for a Culture Mile will bring together the most concentrated cultural offer anywhere.

The *Culture Mile* is a geographic area which joins the new *Museum of London* to the Barbican Centre and the Guildhall School of Music and Drama and which takes in St Paul's Cathedral, Tate Modern and LSO St Luke's. Of course, the City churches, many of them Wren masterpieces, and the beautiful Livery Halls are also used for cultural activities of every variety.

Collectively, these venues and the creative work which goes on within them form an exceptionally attractive addition to London's cultural offering. Not only that but, being as we are in the financial district of the capital, the Arts make an enormous contribution to London's (and the UK's) economy.

We thank Paul Jagger and Julian Cable for pulling together the eclectic mix of material which makes up the first edition of *Songs and Music of the City of London*. We commend the volume to you and ask you to send in your updates so that the authors can make it not only a joy to read but also an accurate work of reference.

Most of all – visit the venues, support the artists, and share the excitement and enjoy!

Sir Andrew Parmley
Lord Mayor 2016–2017
Master Musician 2012–2013
Chief Executive, Royal College of Organists
Honorary Organist, St James, Garlickhythe

About this guide

As with so much else about the City of London, the vast array of City organisations, events, venues, activities and historical links that are associated with songs and music are both in plain sight and earshot (for those who care to look and listen) and yet largely hidden, at least in the sense of providing a readily accessible overview of the topic.

This guide is intended to provide both a broad perspective on the City's musical life and shine a light on each of the many and varied aspects of musical performance, study, sponsorship, training, examination and awarding. It also captures the various songs, hymns and anthems of the City's Livery Companies.

However, this guide is neither a history nor a comprehensive study of the topic – it is simply too vast to capture in concise form.

Some might be surprised to discover that the City has significant musical credentials to speak of at all. Given the City's stature as the world's leading centre for financial and professional services with over half a million office workers in the most economically productive part of the UK, first we should ask the question, 'What has the City of London ever done for music?'

The City's musical credentials

Nobody can be sure when songs and music were first heard in the City of London. The first man-made instruments to be heard in the City were probably the Roman trumpets, cornets and bucines[1] sounded by legionaries as a means of signalling orders. It's likely that the early residents of the City knew martial music as the life of the City followed the political, social and economic structures present elsewhere in the Roman Empire.

In the early 7th century, St Augustine became the inaugural Archbishop of Canterbury and it was during his office that Mellitus became the first post-Roman Bishop of London. It would have been during this period that Gregorian chant was first heard in the City of London.

The City of London has never been afraid to blow its own trumpet and some might say it is to the manner born. The City's civic year begins with the installation of the Lord Mayor, announced to the citizens of London outside Guildhall by a fanfare performed by a detachment of four state trumpeters from the Band of the Household Cavalry– magnificently attired in their gold embroidered tunics. By curious comparison, the installation of the Lord Mayor is held in Guildhall moments before in what is aptly titled 'The Silent Ceremony'.

The world's oldest street pageant is the Lord Mayor's Show, held in the City every year on the second Saturday in November. Anyone who has watched the Show on television or lined the route in the City cannot have missed the enormous array of marching bands that participate. A military band always leads the Show after forming up near Mansion House. Interspersed with the floats representing various civic, corporate and charitable organisations, a wide array of bands representing the Armed Forces, the Scout and Guides Associations, the Boys' Brigade, the Salvation Army and one or more City-affiliated schools are to be found.

---

[1] A kind of great horn shaped in a wide spiral.

So it would seem that the first music heard in the City was martial in nature, and that aspect of City life continues through to the present.

Musicians of the Household Cavalry Band performing in the Lord Mayor's Show
(Copyright Garry Knight, Creative Commons License [2])

The City's musical credentials go far beyond the pomp and pageantry of the Lord Mayor's Show although, as with so much else about the City, the depth and variety of ways in which it is connected with music are truly spectacular yet not widely known outside of professional and church circles. However, they are not all so grand and majestic as the Lord Mayor's Show. For example, the first record of a morris dancing side being employed for entertainment dates back to the 15th century when the Goldsmiths' Company (one of the City's Livery Companies or guilds) paid for morris dancers to attend the Company at its annual St Dunstan's Day service and dinner.

---

[2] https://creativecommons.org/licenses/by-sa/2.0/legalcode

In the late 15th century, the Court of Common Council ordered that the City's several watchmen, known as the City Waits, were to use their pipes and horns to 'walk every night for the recreation of the citizens and to avoid robberies'. By this ordinance the City Waits became as much entertainers as watch keepers. Earlier in the century, the City Waits had received official recognition by the Lord Mayor and Aldermen, and were permitted to wear a Livery (uniform) like the members of the City Companies. How this proto-Livery Company for Music related to the Society of Minstrels – now the Worshipful Company of Musicians – is unknown. The City Waits are no longer with us, and perhaps that's because their musical accomplishments were not of the highest order; one report describes their noise as sounding like 'the Devil riding or hunting through the City'. No such accusation could be levelled at the modern incarnation – The City Musick – mentioned elsewhere in this guide!

Musical performances also got an early commercial foothold in the City when the world's first music concerts, to which the public were admitted on payment of a shilling, were held in 1672 in the home of John Banister –one of 24 violinists to Charles II. Samuel Pepys wrote of Banister's anger when the King replaced him with a French musician.

The Polish composer Frederic Chopin gave his final public performance on 16 November 1848 during an event that was jointly organised by the Court of Common Council (The City's governing body) and the Literary Association of the Friends of Poland in order to raise funds for Polish refugees in London.

The City is best known for its financial and professional services firms, and for being the original Roman heart of what is now Greater London; yet the City is also a major sponsor of the arts and has a bewildering array of professional, semi-professional and voluntary organisations variously engaged in performance, education or support of songs and music. During the writing of this guide a new exhibition titled *The London Jukebox* opened in the London Mithraeum, the last work of the late Susan Hiller, an American artist who was resident in London for most of her life. The Jukebox captures 70 popular songs about London that Susan gathered over a 10-year period up to 2018. This contemporary art installation has been described as a form of archaeology, albeit one that is very much there to be experienced in modern times.

The COVID-19 pandemic has been a hugely challenging time for music and for the livelihood of musicians, with live performances all but suspended. While being no full substitute for the interaction between performers and a live audience, modern technology has enabled some organisations and venues to broadcast concerts or religious services online, either live-streamed or with pre-recorded music, being performed with a significantly reduced or no live audience or congregation present. By using an online platform such as YouTube, some events have attracted far larger audiences than would ever be possible for a physical event, unconstrained by geographic location or the need to listen at a specific time.

Of particular note, in December 2020 the City rose to the challenge of engaging a remote audience in what must have been one of the largest virtual carol services ever conducted when 5,000 participants from all over the world attended a *Carols for the City* live event opened by HRH Prince Edward, Earl of Wessex KG KCVO, and the Lord Mayor. The service, which was sponsored by London Wall Partners, raised over £50,000 for the VOCES8 Foundation; The charity of the Worshipful Company of Information Technologists (WCIT Charity); the Lord Mayor's Appeal; and the Friends of City Churches. It was organised by the Information Technologists' Company and the VOCES8 Foundation from whose base in the Church of St Anne and St Agnes (in Gresham Street) the service was streamed. It stands as testimony to the City's ability to innovate: blending technology with song and music in aid of a charitable cause.

During the pandemic, national lockdown in the winter of 2020–2021, the Worshipful Company of Architects in partnership with the Temple

Bar Trust commissioned a series of videos about the City's built environment and its connections with composers. The project is titled *Founded on Music: 1000 years building the City of London*. We hope that the City's resurgence after the pandemic is similarly founded on music.

As the world emerges from the grip of COVID-19, we can look forward to a resurgence of musical events in the City. This publication is designed to be a useful pocket guide, and to that end it brings together the organisation, characters, events and just a little of the history of the Square Mile's musical life into a harmonious yet compact concert of information that will aid anyone with an interest in songs and music of the City.

City venues for music

The City of London is surprisingly well served for musical venues, including most of the City's churches, several of the Livery Halls and, especially, the Barbican Centre. While the Barbican Centre is the City's only purpose-built venue for music, there is no shortage of smaller settings where the public can enjoy performances often at little or no cost.

The City's churches warrant particular attention as venues for public performance of music and worship. Therefore, the numerous churches and their musical connections are covered in a chapter of their own.

Barbican Centre

Web: https://www.barbican.org.uk/
Twitter: @BarbicanCentre

World-famous for its artistic programming and iconic architecture, the Barbican Centre is located within the Barbican Estate, the City's largest residential estate. The name derives from the former defensive forecastle outside the City's western gates, and the arts centre was opened in 1982 by the Queen, who described it as 'one of the wonders of the modern world'.

The Barbican Centre is part of the City of London Corporation – the City's local government authority. The City of London Corporation is the fourth greatest sponsor of the arts in the United Kingdom (after the Government, the BBC, and the National Lottery), with the Barbican Centre the most obvious manifestation of the City's support for arts and culture.

Within the cavernous space of the Barbican Centre is a concert hall with capacity for almost 2,000 people, as well as two theatres, two art galleries, cinemas, public spaces, a library, and a glasshouse conservatory. The Barbican is also home to the London Symphony Orchestra (LSO), with Sir Simon Rattle as its current Music Director.

The Barbican Centre's entrance on Silk Street sets the tone for the brutalist architecture of the venue
(Photo © Paul D Jagger)

Other orchestras, choirs, and ensembles that are associated with the Barbican include the BBC Symphony Orchestra, the Academy of Ancient Music, the Britten Sinfonia, and several international orchestras.

During the COVID-19 pandemic, the Barbican ran a number of virtual events, including Soundhouse, a platform for creative radio and podcasting. Soundhouse created a shared experience among listeners by delivering 'looping' radio broadcasts that could be listened to online. Music performances were also live streamed from the Barbican Hall with socially distanced musicians and audiences as part of the *Live from the Barbican* concert series.

The London Symphony Orchestra (LSO), under Music Director Sir Simon Rattle, performing at the Barbican Hall
(Photo by Mark Allan, courtesy of the LSO)

The Barbican's international arts programme spans the art forms and includes an immense array of concerts encompassing classical, modern, and experimental musical performances. The latest list of events may be viewed and booked via the Barbican website.

The Barbican Centre also operates a membership scheme. Members get access to the Member Lounge; benefit from priority booking; save on booking fees; and receive a 20% discount on selected tickets. Additional benefits are available at the Member Plus level. There is also a Young Barbican scheme to which persons aged 14-25 may subscribe. Full details on the Barbican website.

St Bride's Foundation

Web: https://www.sbf.org.uk
Twitter: @StBrideLibrary

Home to the Bridewell Theatre and venue for musical performances, St Bride's Foundation also runs a wide range of workshops. The St Bride's Foundation is a cultural and social charity with an education mission. It celebrated its 125th anniversary in 2020.

The Charterhouse

Web: https://thecharterhouse.org
Twitter: @CharterhouseEC1

Sutton's Hospital at Charterhouse, while in the London Borough of Islington, is inextricably linked with the City of London and was once the home of the prestigious Charterhouse School – now moved to Godalming in Surrey. The Charterhouse was originally a monastic institution and is now an almshouse. It has long admitted musicians among its Brothers – a term that now includes female as well as male residents.

An early musician Captain Tobias Hume (1579–1645) spent the last 13 years of his life as a 'Poor Brother' at the Charterhouse. A notorious prankster, among his many works was a piece entitled *An Invention for Two to Play upon One Viole.*

Another notable musician with connection to the Charterhouse was Dr Johann Christoph Pepusch, who was organist from 1737 to 1753. Pepusch was one of several notable 18th-century musicians, along with Handel and J.C. Bach, who came originally from mainland Europe and then settled in London for most of their working lives. In 1725, Pepusch founded what became the Academy of Ancient Music (originally the Academy of Vocal Music).

The Charterhouse is also a venue for music, boasting a Great Hall, and a Great Chamber that underwent significant refurbishment in 2020. In addition to the Charterhouse's public tours, a series of regular events are advertised, including an annual carol service.

Charterhouse has hosted the Sound Unbound festival in partnership with Culture Mile, featuring a programme of early English music including The Academy of Ancient Music, often with a modern twist.

Drapers' Hall

Web: https://www.thedrapers.co.uk/

The Worshipful Company of Drapers is one of the City's Twelve Great Livery Companies. Its hall is regularly ranked as one of the most magnificent venues in the Square Mile and stood in for Buckingham Palace in the film *The King's Speech*.

The hall provides a spectacular venue for concerts as it has a variety of well-suited, spacious rooms. It is regularly used for corporate and Livery events. Since the mid-1990s, the Company has hosted concerts performed by the various London conservatoires that it supports.

LSO St Luke's

Web: https://lso.co.uk/lso-st-lukes.html
Twitter: @londonsymphony

The London Symphony Orchestra maintains a music education centre
and venue for hire just outside the City in the St Luke's centre in Old
Street. St Luke's was an abandoned church until it was converted to a
dedicated centre for musical education in 2000; the LSO moved in and
performed its first concert in 2003.

LSO St Luke's is now the venue for regular performances including BBC
Radio 3 lunchtime concerts, which are then broadcast on air and on the
BBC website. The LSO also performs a series of free Friday lunchtime
concerts.

Merchant Taylors' Hall

Web: https://www.merchant-taylors.co.uk/
Twitter: @merchanttaylor1

It is believed that the first time the British National Anthem was sung (then, "God save great George our King") was in Merchant Taylors' Hall.

Uniquely among Livery Company halls, Merchant Taylors' Hall has a working organ. It was the last organ to be built by Renatus Harris, in 1722, originally for the church of St Dionis Backchurch (later demolished). The current organ in the hall was installed in 1966. It was built by Noel Mander and incorporated much of the pipework from Harris' organ. John Dykes Bower, then organist of St Paul's Cathedral, gave an inaugural concert the following year.

In addition to music performed for corporate and Livery Company events, Merchant Taylors' Hall also hosts an annual concert performed by musicians from Merchant Taylors' School.

Middle Temple Hall

Web: https://www.middletemplevenue.org.uk

The Inns of Court were modelled on the City's Livery Companies from their earliest foundation. Among them the Honourable Society of the Middle Temple's Hall is often used as a venue for musical performances, especially in partnership with the Temple Music Foundation.

The Belcea Quartet playing in Middle Temple
(Photo courtesy of the Honourable Society of the Middle Temple)

Salters' Hall

Web: https://www.salters.co.uk/
Twitter: @SaltersCompany

Among the many magnificent Livery Halls in the City of London, Salters' Hall on Fore Street is known for its acoustic qualities. The exterior of the hall mirrors the Brutalist architecture of the Barbican Estate which surrounds it on three sides; yet the interior is a cavernous space panelled in a mellow golden ribbed wood and well designed to carry sound from a minstrels' gallery above the main dining room. The hall was originally designed by Sir Basil Spence in 1967. A remodelling in the 21st century has resulted in a venue that does credit to the Company and would not look out of place in the nearby Barbican Centre.

Perhaps it is this suitability to the performance of music that attracted the Associated Board of the Royal Schools of Music (ABRSM) to move to offices in Salters' Hall in 2015. See the separate entry for ABRSM elsewhere in this guide.

A sense of the acoustic qualities of Salters' Hall may be experienced by watching the short YouTube video clip *Fanfare for a Dignified Occasion* on the website of London Fanfare Trumpets.

Stationers' Hall

Web: https://stationershall.co.uk
Twitter: @StationersHall

The Stationers & Newspaper Makers' Company boasts a magnificent hall a stone's throw from St Paul's Cathedral. The hall is regularly leased for private and corporate events and its main dining hall has excellent acoustic qualities. Unsurprisingly, it is a popular venue for all manner of musical performances.

It is noteworthy that Stationers' Hall features a magnificent stained-glass window depicting a scene with St Cecilia, who is the Patron Saint of Music and Musicians. The Company also manages the adjacent church of St Martin within Ludgate.

Tower Bridge

Web: https://www.towerbridge.org.uk/
Twitter: @TowerBridge

An uplifting venue that raises music to new heights or, more precisely, to new depths because Tower Bridge is the unusual setting for the annual Bascule Chamber Concerts, part of the Totally Thames festival. The concerts are composed and curated by the appropriately named musician Iain Chambers.

The Bascule Chamber is the hidden space that the bridge's counterweights occupy when the bridge is raised. The dramatic brick-lined space is below the level of the Thames and is atmospherically lit to emphasise the cavernous nature of this dramatic domain.

Details of the Bascule Chamber Concerts and other events held in Tower Bridge may be found on the bridge's website.

Music in City churches and other places of worship

Despite the Great Fire and the Blitz, the City is still blessed with more than 40 churches, some of which have Norman origins; most standing today were rebuilt or substantially restored by Sir Christopher Wren and his protégé Nicholas Hawksmoor. Because of their prominent and longstanding role in the musical life of the City, the churches warrant coverage in somewhat more depth than the other topics in this guide.

The importance of worship and faith in the Square Mile is explored in the book *Faith in the City of London* by Niki Gorick, published in 2020.

The publication *City Events* by the Friends of the City Churches in conjunction with the Archdeaconry of London, provides details of events, including musical ones, at these churches.

A full exploration of their contribution, past and present, is beyond the scope of this guide.

Several of the City's churches and other places of worship host regular recitals and services. Some notable examples are described here.

St Paul's Cathedral

Web: https://www.stpauls.co.uk
Twitter: @StPaulsLondon

Director of Music: Andrew Carwood (since 2007)

A cathedral dedicated to St Paul has stood on the site, the highest in the City of London, for at least 1400 years. The current building, at least the fourth, was the masterpiece of Sir Christopher Wren following the destruction of its predecessor in the Great Fire of London in 1666.

The Cathedral's daily round of worship is led by a renowned choir of men and boys. The choristers of St Paul's Cathedral are educated at St Paul's Cathedral School, an independent school which is located adjacent to the Cathedral, founded originally in 1123 and refounded in 1874.

Music has featured prominently at the numerous major national occasions that St Paul's Cathedral has hosted through history, including the state funeral of Sir Winston Churchill in 1965; the wedding of HRH the Prince of Wales and Lady Diana Spencer in 1981; the Diamond Jubilee of HM The Queen in 2012; and the funeral of Baroness Thatcher in 2013.

To accompany the choir is a fine five-manual organ and sometimes an orchestra to accompany a Mass setting. The organ was originally built by Bernard Smith in 1694, with an organ case unusually designed by the architect (Wren). The organ was subsequently modified and enlarged by Willis and Mander. It has a versatile array of stops including, high above the west door, three Royal Trumpets that are shown off to impressive effect on special occasions and celebrity recitals alike.

Back in the 16th century, the choristers not only sang at the Cathedral services but, together with boys of the Chapel Royal, they had parallel roles in theatrical court performances, including in competition with the works of Shakespeare, which took place in locations that included Greenwich, Hampton Court, Windsor Castle, Globe Theatre, and King's College Chapel, Cambridge.

The musical standards at the Cathedral were not always as high as in the present day. In the middle of the 19th century, the standard of singing was considered to be poor, but enjoyed a notable subsequent revival in the 1870s after John Stainer was appointed organist. Chorister numbers increased to almost 40 and the new school in Carter Lane was built.

Today, tours to new and sometimes far-flung destinations are a regular feature in the life of a cathedral or church choir. In 1953, the St Paul's choir undertook a ground-breaking tour to the USA and Canada, which was the first time in 800 years of history that they sang outside London. The tour marked the building of the American Memorial Chapel in honour of the 28,000 US servicemen who gave their lives in the Second World War. Lasting memories from choristers included trying to smuggle a deadly black widow spider, live in a glass jar, onto a Qantas flight home.

In 2016, a Diamond Fund Jubilee Concert was held, at which choristers from almost every UK cathedral took part. The concert marked the 60th anniversary of the Friends of Cathedral Music, an organisation dedicated to promoting music in British cathedrals and awarding funds for choirs in need.

The choir of St Paul's Cathedral, under their Director of Music, Andrew Carwood, at a service of Choral Evensong
(Photo © Chapter of St Paul's. Photo by Graham Lacdao)

At some other occasions, combined choirs sing at St Paul's. At the annual Festival of St Cecilia – the patron saint of music – the choirs of St Paul's, Westminster Abbey and Westminster Cathedral sing together, including a new anthem composed for each year's service. Also, two other cathedral choirs (changing each year) join the St Paul's choir to sing at the Festival of the Clergy Support Trust (formerly the Sons and Friends of the Clergy) which, since 1655, has supported the families of destitute clergy members, originally those who were deprived of their income during the time of Oliver Cromwell as Lord Protector.

In 2017, history was made when Sir Andrew Parmley, the first music teacher and organist to be elected Lord Mayor of London, performed at the Cathedral as the soloist in Saint-Saëns' Organ Symphony, in a concert in aid of the Lord Mayor's Appeal.

Andrew Carwood is the first non-organist to hold the post of Director of Music since the 12th century, having established a reputation as a choral conductor – including as Director of The Cardinall's Musick – and as a singer.

Did you know? Each of the choristers of St Paul's Cathedral Choir is sponsored by a City of London Livery Company. The chorister's sponsoring company can be determined from the medal they wear.

Temple Church

Web: http://www.templechurch.com
Twitter: @TempleChurchLDN

Director of Music: Roger Sayer (since 2013)

Of the four Inns of Court, two of them – Inner Temple and Middle Temple – are within the City of London but are not subject to the writ of the Lord Mayor. This area, known as the Temple, was named after the Knights Templar, who first occupied the site in the 12th century. Under the Templars, the church already had organs and a choir of men and boys.

At Middle Temple, musical and theatrical entertainment – especially around the Christmas season – was a typical feature of life at the Inn. In 1602, the first performance of Shakespeare's *Twelfth Night* was given in Middle Temple Hall. A few years later, masques designed by Inigo Jones were performed.

The Temple Church, originally the church of the soldier monks, dates from 1185. It is not only one of London's oldest churches but also one of only four round churches in England. Magna Carta was negotiated in the Temple between November 1214 and May 1215. From the Temple the London Charter was issued in May 1215, empowering the City to elect its own Lord Mayor, who must then be presented to the Lord Chief

Justice. This Charter, still in force, is the reason for the procession of the Lord Mayor's Show to the Royal Courts of Justice. Magna Carta's hero, William Marshal, is buried in the Temple's Round where his effigy still lies.

The musical fame of the Temple Church was sealed in 1927 when the boy chorister Ernest Lough made his renowned recording of the solo "O, for the Wings of a Dove" from Mendelssohn's anthem *Hear my prayer*. At that time, 700,000 copies of the recording were sold– a record number – and it is still available today. Such was the level of interest that for many months after the recording was made, queues of people wanting to attend the Sunday morning service went all around the Temple Church and onto Fleet Street. Lough was accompanied by Dr George Thalben-Ball (known to choristers affectionately as 'The Doctor'), who was Temple organist and choirmaster for almost six decades, retiring in 1982 not far short of his 90th birthday.

The church's services (Sundays at 11:15 AM and Wednesdays at 5:45 PM) are sung by the men and boys of the Temple Church Choir and the men and women of the Temple Singers. Both choirs also give regular concerts. There are frequent recitals (most Wednesdays at 1:15 PM) on the four-manual Harrison & Harrison organ, on which Roger Sayer played the soundtrack to Interstellar.

The Temple Church Choir has had close links with the City of London School for Boys since 1900.

See also 'Temple Music Foundation'.

City Temple

Web: https://www.city-temple.com
Twitter: @City_Temple

City Temple, on Holborn Viaduct, is home to the oldest Nonconformist congregation in the City of London, believed to have been founded in 1640. The church building is from 1874 and was rebuilt following war damage in 1958.

An organ by Forster & Andrews of Hull was installed in 1876. In 1926, it was rebuilt and incorporated some pipes from the old Norman & Beard organ from Jesus College Chapel, Cambridge. In 1958, following the postwar rebuilding, a new Walker organ was installed.

Mercers' Company Chapel

Web: https://www.mercers.co.uk

The Worshipful Company of Mercers (the name 'Mercer' being derived from the Latin *mercator*, a merchant) is first in the order of precedence of City of London Livery Companies, and is the only one to have a hall with its own private chapel. Gilbert Becket, the father of Archbishop Thomas Becket, had a shop on the site of the present hall in Ironmonger Lane, and Thomas' sister and her husband founded the hospital of St Thomas of Acon on the site. In 1538, the premises were bought by Sir Thomas Gresham (founder of Gresham College) for the Mercers' Company, and the hospital church became the Company chapel. The current hall is the third one, which opened in 1958 after being rebuilt following wartime destruction.

In 1867, an organ was installed in the Mercers' chapel. Dating from 1710, it was made for the Chapel Royal at St James' and was then in the Episcopal Chapel in Long Acre. In 1883, it was replaced in the Mercers' chapel by a new Bevington instrument. That instrument was destroyed in the Blitz in 1941, and was replaced by a Walker organ when the hall was rebuilt in 1958.

All Hallows by the Tower (or All Hallows Barking)

Web: https://www.ahbtt.org.uk
Twitter: @AllHallowsTower

Director of Music: Jonathan Melling

The church of All Hallows by the Tower claims to be the oldest church in the City of London, dating from AD 675.

Some notable people who were beheaded at the Tower of London are buried at the church, including Archbishop William Laud, Thomas More, and John Fisher.

Albert Schweitzer, theologian and philosopher, made organ recordings at the church. The current organ was built by Harrison & Harrison in 1957. A regular programme of Thursday lunchtime organ recitals takes place.

Concerts occasionally take place with other performing groups, such as the East London Chorus and singers from City Music Services.

Each June, the Knollys Rose Ceremony begins here, in which a rose is carried in procession on an altar cushion from All Hallows by the Tower to Mansion House.

All Hallows London (or All Hallows-on-the-Wall)

Web: http://www.london-city-churches.org.uk/Churches/
AllHallowsontheWall/index.html

This church's name refers to its location beside London Wall, the former city wall. The present building dates from 1767. It is a guild church of the Worshipful Company of Carpenters. It was formerly the headquarters of the Council for the Care of Churches and then of Christian Aid. Since 2017, it has housed the urban youth charity XLP, and is visited annually by the Duke and Duchess of Cambridge.

The church has records of an organ being installed as early as 1509, replacing a former one. The current organ was installed in 1962 following wartime damage repairs to the church. This Hill organ was moved from its previous home at Manor House in Highbury by Mander, who made some changes to the instrument.

Bevis Marks Synagogue

Web: https://www.sephardi.org.uk/bevis-marks
Twitter: @sandpuk

A body of Jewish settlers arrived in England with the Norman Conquest in 1066. The Jews were then expelled in the reign of Edward I in 1290. They did not return until three and a half centuries later. In the intervening period, the Jews from the Sephardic community in Europe escaped from Spain, as a result of the Spanish Inquisition, first to Portugal, and later migrated to Holland.

In 1656, a group of Jewish settlers arrived in London from Amsterdam, with the agreement of Oliver Cromwell. The Jews in England were now permitted to practise their faith openly, and Bevis Marks Synagogue was built in response to this need, within walking distance of where they lived.

Bevis Marks Synagogue was completed in 1701. The building was modelled on the synagogue in Amsterdam and also influenced by the style of the City churches being built at the time in the aftermath of the Great Fire of London. Bevis Marks is the oldest continuously used synagogue in the UK. It is affiliated to the Spanish and Portuguese (Sephardic) Jewish community.

Out of any City places of worship, the original interior of Bevis Marks Synagogue has remained the most untouched. One change that did occur was the addition of choir stalls in the early to mid-19th century. It was not a custom for a choir to sing in the synagogue at the time it was built; that situation changed a century later.

Choral music sung in the synagogue might include traditional Sephardi melodies that are harmonised, possibly by the choirmaster, to suit the location where they are sung – in this case, in a westernised style.

In Sephardic worship, the choir and reader lead the congregation. The Sephardi community has published online recordings of London Sephardi congregational melodies. These recordings were prepared by Eliot Alderman, formerly Director of Music to the Spanish and Portuguese Jews' Congregation, and Rabbi Jonathan Cohen, former Visiting Rabbi of Bevis Marks Synagogue. The aim is to encourage congregants and visitors to join in the various sung parts of synagogue worship with confidence.

Charterhouse Chapel

Web: http://www.thecharterhouse.org/explore-the-charterhouse/chapel

Twitter: @CharterhouseEC1

Organist: Graham Matthews

The Charterhouse is a former Carthusian monastery near the Barbican and Smithfield Market. It is now an almshouse, whose community residents, including the current organist, are known as 'Brothers'. The boys' school formerly on the site is now at Godalming in Surrey.

The Chapel holds daily services according to the Book of Common Prayer, with hymns on Sunday.

Christ Church, Spitalfields

Web: https://www.christchurchspitalfields.org/organ

Christ Church, Spitalfields, close to the eastern border of the City of London, is a church designed by Nicholas Hawksmoor. The church organ, built by Richard Bridge in 1735, is of huge significance, it being the largest in the country when built and remaining so for over a century. The organ was restored by William Drake in 2014, and is now regularly used for recitals of organ music, especially from the 18th century.

The Dutch Church

Web: https://www.dutchchurch.org.uk
Twitter: @dutchchurch

Organist: David Titterington (since 1989; Director of Music since 1992)

The Dutch Church, Austin Friars, was established in 1550 for Protestant refugees. It is the world's oldest Dutch-language Protestant church and is regarded as the mother church for Dutch reformed churches.

The current organ, from 1954, was built by the Dutch organ builders, Willem van Leeuwen of Leiderdorp. It is set on a small gallery on the north wall, accessed via a spiral staircase.

St Alban the Martyr, Holborn

Web: https://www.stalbansholborn.co.uk
Twitter: @stalbansholborn

Organist: Edward Batting (since 1998)

This red-brick church was designed in 1859 by William Butterfield, a Gothic Revival architect who also designed Keble College, Oxford and the church of All Saints, Margaret Street in London. St Alban the Martyr was the first Anglican church to hold a three-hour devotion at the foot of the cross on Good Friday, from 1864.

Here, in 1938, the composer Olivier Messiaen gave the first performance in England of his own organ suite, *La Nativité du Seigneur*.

The church's original organ was built by Father Willis in 1893. The present three-manual Compton organ was built in 1961 and sits in the west gallery. The church also has a Lamdin organ, one of Peter Collins' earliest instruments, built in 2004.

St Andrew Holborn

Web: https://www.standrewholborn.org.uk
Twitter: @StAndrewHolborn

Director of Music: James McVinnie

Records of this church date back to the 950s. Following the Blitz, the church was restored to Sir Christopher Wren's previous design. Since the 1960s, the church has functioned as a guild church to serve the local working population.

The organ, in the west gallery, was built by Mander in 1989. It is housed in an 18th-century casing that was designed by Handel for the Foundling Hospital.

Past organists include Daniel Purcell, Maurice Greene, and John Stanley.

St Andrew Undershaft

The church, situated on St Mary Axe, survived both the Great Fire of London and the Blitz. The present building dates from 1532. It is now administered from the nearby St Helen's Bishopsgate.

The organ is historically significant and was built by Renatus Harris in 1696. It has undergone various repairs including by Hill in the 19th century and Walker in the 20th century. The organ was awarded a Grade I historic organ certificate by the British Institute of Organ Studies.

Fabian Stedman (1640–1713), a key figure in the early development of the change ringing system used in church bellringing, is buried at this church.

St Andrew-by-the-Wardrobe

Web: https://www.standrewbythewardrobe.org
Twitter: @bythewardrobe

The church dates back to at least 1170. In the Middle Ages it was part of the royal residence of Baynard's Castle. In 1361, Edward III moved his Royal Wardrobe of clothing and other items from the Tower of London to this location, hence the church's name. William Shakespeare was once a parishioner. The church was rebuilt by Wren in 1695 following the Great Fire of London, and again in 1961 following the Blitz.

The church's first organ was installed in 1774. It was replaced in the 19th century by a Gray instrument, which was rebuilt by Hill. This instrument was destroyed in an air raid in 1940. In 1962, after the church's rebuilding, Mander installed a chamber organ by Snetzler which was rescued from Teddesley Hall in Staffordshire; it is a valuable, unaltered 18th-century instrument.

St Anne and St Agnes

Web: http://www.greshamcentre.com/st-anne-and-st-agnes-church

A church has been present on the site since at least 1137. It was rebuilt by Wren following the Great Fire of London, and again following destruction from the Blitz. From 1966 to 2013 it was used by Lutheran exiled Estonian and Latvian communities. Since 2013, it has been known as the Gresham Centre. It houses the VOCES8 vocal octet ensemble and their education project, Voces Cantabiles Music. VOCES8 and other groups give occasional concerts at the church.

The Priory Church of St Bartholomew the Great, and St Bartholomew the Less

Web: https://www.greatstbarts.com
Twitter: @StBartholomews

Director of Music: Rupert Gough (since 2015)

St Bartholomew the Great lays claim to being London's oldest parish church, dating from 1123. Its smaller neighbour, St Bartholomew the Less, was a separate parish until the two parishes were merged in 2015.

At St Bartholomew the Great, the main church choir consists of professional singers. The church has a scholarship scheme with the Royal Holloway College, whereby four singers receive a stipend and sing at services in term time, and are mentored by current choir members.

The choir, directed by Rupert Gough, and congregation of St Bartholomew the
Great at a church service
(Photo courtesy of the Rector, the Reverend Marcus Walker)

The original organ was built by John Knopple in 1715. The church is in the process of acquiring a new organ. It will replace a previous organ that was purchased from St Stephen Walbrook in 1885 and overhauled by Mander and Wells. A list of the church's organists going back to 1715 includes a few female organists from the mid-19th century.

In 1794, at St Bartholomew the Less, an organ was installed in the place of the former Treasurer's pew. It was replaced by a Gray organ in 1825, a Gray & Davison organ in 1863, a Hill, Norman & Beard organ in 1930 and a Mander organ in 1971.

The Priory Church hosts services for associated organisations throughout the year, including for several City Livery Companies. The church is the home of the City Music Society, whose Trust is run by Leslie East.

In the 1950s, Dr Paul Steinitz, then Director of Music, gave the first British performance of the complete Bach's St Matthew Passion sung in German, with his London Bach Society.

During the 1970s, Andrew Morris, then Director of Music, organised an ambitious regular schedule of music festivals, organ recitals, and other concerts at the church, in collaboration with the then Rector, the Reverend Prebendary Dr Newell Wallbank. The festivals included one in 1973 to mark 850 years since the church's foundation, and one in 1977 for the Queen's Silver Jubilee. An International Festival of Twentieth Century Music was held in 1978, with HM Queen Elizabeth The Queen Mother as Patron, and additional patronage from such musical luminaries as Sir Lennox Berkeley, Sir Adrian Boult, Mrs Ralph Vaughan Williams, and Sir Peter Pears. One concert in 1979 gave the first London performance of all the sequenzas that Luciano Berio had composed to date.

In 1973, for the 850th anniversary of St Bartholomew's Hospital and St Bartholomew the Great, the composer Donald Swann (of Flanders and

Swann fame) composed a song especially for the occasion: *The Song of the Building*.

In 2019, the church inaugurated a monthly *Evensong in the City* service on a Thursday, inviting City workers to sing in a specially convened choir at the service – followed by bangers and mash served in the cloister!

In 2020, after easing of the first COVID-19 lockdown restrictions, St Bartholomew the Great was one of the first London churches to resume choral evensong with a live choir, socially distanced, on the occasion of its Patronal Festival in August 2020. During subsequent lockdown and its gradual easing in 2021, the church was a pioneer in providing pre-recorded or livestreamed services online, and then in welcoming back an in-person congregation, in accordance with the prevailing regulations.

Did you know? *Four Weddings and a Funeral* was filmed in 1994 at the Priory Church (for wedding number four), and it has been a popular venue for weddings ever since.

St Benet Paul's Wharf

Web: http://www.stbenetwelshchurch.org.uk
Twitter: @stbenetswelsh

St Benet Paul's Wharf is a Welsh Anglican church and holds a Sunday morning service in Welsh, with English translation provided. It is also the official church of the College of Arms.

The current church was designed by Wren and escaped damage in the Second World War.

The first organ was built by Bishop in 1832. The current instrument, also in the west gallery, was built in 1973 by Hill, Norman and Beard, salvaging some material from a fire two years earlier.

St Botolph Aldersgate (or St Botolph without Aldersgate)

Web: https://www.stbotolphsaldersgate.org.uk

This church was one of four medieval churches at the City gates dedicated to St Botolph, who was the patron saint of travellers.

It is now a guild church serving the weekday population. Sunday services are held here by the London City Presbyterian Church.

The west gallery organ was built by Samuel Green in 1788.

The Amati Orchestra rehearses here.

St Botolph Aldgate (or St Botolph without Aldgate)

Web: https://www.stbotolphs.org.uk
Twitter: @BotolphAldgate

Director of Music and Choirmaster: Shanna Hart

The organ is arguably the oldest surviving church organ in England. It was built by Renatus Harris in 1704 and has the oldest collection of pipes in their original positions. The organ was subsequently enlarged and restored several times, most recently by Goetze & Gwynn in 2006.

Today, Wednesday lunchtime recitals are held, and regularly feature the organ. The church also has a rare Schimmel grand piano.

The current Director of Music was a recent Organ Scholar at Selwyn College, Cambridge.

St Botolph Bishopsgate (or St Botolph without Bishopsgate)

Web:　　http://www.botolph.org.uk
Twitter: @botolph_s

Director of Music: Iestyn Evans

St Botolph sits just outside (or 'without') Bishopsgate, the former eastern gate to the City of London. Next to the churchyard's Bishopsgate entrance is a memorial cross thought to be the first memorial to the First World War erected in the country. Next to the church are the former course of London Wall, and a Turkish bath dating from 1895.

The church has a choir of professional singers, who sing at a weekly Eucharist service on Wednesdays at 1:10 PM. Before that service, the church's set of eight bells are rung. The church is also a venue for concerts.

An organ was built in 1764, and was enlarged in the following century by Henry Willis and again in 1949, preserving some 1764 pipework. The organ was damaged in the IRA bomb explosion in 1994 and subsequently restored.

St Bride

Web: http://www.stbrides.com
Twitter: @stbrideschurch

Director of Music: Robert Jones (since 1988)

St Bride's Church, in Fleet Street, has long been associated with journalists and the newspaper trade.

The present building, at least the seventh on the site, was designed by Sir Christopher Wren in 1672, following the destruction of its predecessor during the Great Fire of London six years earlier.

The church has a notable tower and spire; the tower was the site of the first ever full peal rung on 12 bells, and the spire was the inspiration for the first tiered wedding cake.

Notable former parishioners included the 17th-century poets, John Milton and John Dryden, and the diarist, Samuel Pepys. Polly Nichols, the first known victim of Jack the Ripper, grew up in the parish, and was married at St Bride's in 1864. Her life is commemorated by a plaque inside the west door.

Since the rededication of the church in 1957 following restoration from damage in the Blitz, the choir has been formed of 12 adult professional singers who sing at two services each Sunday and for other special services. The organ is a versatile four-manual instrument built by the John Compton Organ Company (who also built the famed cinema organ at the Odeon, Leicester Square).

The early 17th-century composer Thomas Weelkes is buried in the crypt, and Henry Purcell's *Te Deum* and *Jubilat*e were first performed in the church in 1694. This was part of the annual St Cecilia Festival sponsored by the Stationers' Company, with whom the church still enjoys close links. The John Armitage Memorial Trust (JAM), which commissions and performs new music, holds an annual concert here, as does EC4 Music, an organisation representing businesses in the Fleet Street area. Regular lunchtime concerts and recitals are held on Tuesdays and Fridays throughout much of the year.

Choristers of the Guild of St Bride
(Photo courtesy of the Revd Canon Dr Alison Joyce, Rector of St Bride's Church)

St Clement Danes

Web: https://stclementdanesraf.org
Twitter: @DanesChurch

St Clement Danes was designed by Sir Christopher Wren and is one of two island churches on the Strand. It is the principal church of the Royal Air Force.

The bands of the Royal Air Force play at services and ceremonies for the RAF and its associated organisations.

The current organ was built by Harrison & Harrison in 1958, and was a gift from the United States Air Force. The organ case is a replica from the Father Smith organ of 1690.

Professor Martindale Sidwell (also formerly organist of Hampstead Parish Church) was organist of St Clement Danes for 35 years until 1992.

St Clement Eastcheap

Organist: Ian Shaw (since 2008)

St Clement Eastcheap claims to be the church referred to in the first line of the nursery rhyme, *Oranges and Lemons,* "Say the bells of St Clements". However, other churches were closer to the River Thames, where fruit might have been unloaded on its way to Leadenhall Market. The author of the rhyme might have chosen the name St Clements primarily for its consonance with the word 'lemons'.

The church's organ preserves its oak case from the Renatus Harris organ built in 1696. The instrument has been rebuilt and restored many times since then, including by Abraham Jordan (1711), who likely added the swell organ; Gray and Davidson (1872), who moved the organ from the west gallery to the south aisle; J.W. Walker (1926); and Hill, Norman and Beard (1936), who moved it back to a west-end location, and later made tonal revisions (1971).

Notable organists at the church include Edward Purcell (son of Henry Purcell) and Jonathan Battishill.

St Dunstan in the West

Web: https://www.stdunstaninthewest.org
Twitter: @Saint_Dunstan

The original church was medieval, before being demolished in the early 19th century to make way for the widening of Fleet Street, and was then rebuilt.

It is shared with the Romanian Orthodox community.

The church holds lunchtime recitals, usually on a Wednesday. The local choir, Chantage, sings at major church festivals.

Did you know? St Dunstan is the patron saint of the Worshipful Company of Goldsmiths.

St Edmund, King and Martyr

Web: https://www.lombardchurches.org

This church, in Lombard Street, now houses the London Centre for Spiritual Direction.

The church's first organ was built by Renatus Harris in 1702. It was rebuilt by Bishop in 1833 and again by others later in the 19th century.

Following bomb damage in 1917, the organ was repaired by Harrison & Harrison. It was rebuilt by Compton in 1934. It was renovated in 1969 through the generosity of Barclays Bank.

Did you know? The church is named after the Anglo-Saxon King who was killed during a Viking raid near what is now Bury St Edmunds. The site of his burial became an Abbey which was the venue for the negotiations that led to Magna Carta being sealed at Runnymede in 1215 AD.

St Etheldreda, Ely Place

Web: http://www.stetheldreda.com

Director of Music: Stuart Kale

This Roman Catholic church survives from the reign of Edward I in the late 13th century, where it served as the town chapel for the Bishops of Ely – the diocese of which has St Etheldreda as its patron saint. The church once served as an embassy chapel for the Spanish Ambassador. It holds the unusual annual sacrament of the Blessing of the Throats.

It has a professional choir that sings at Latin Mass (Renaissance, Viennese, and other settings) on Sundays and major feast days.

St Giles Cripplegate (or St Giles without Cripplegate)

Web: https://www.stgilesnewsite.co.uk
Twitter: @stgilescg

Director of Music: Anne Marsden Thomas (since 1980)

This ancient church, damaged by fire several times and then rebuilt, now sits within the modern Barbican Centre complex. The author John Milton was buried here in 1674.

The current Director of Music is a widely renowned organ performer, teacher, examiner, and author of books for organists. She founded the St Giles International Organ School in 1992 and was a long-time Director of the Royal College of Organists' RCO Academy Summer Course.

St Giles has three organs: The Grand Organ – a restored Mander three-manual gallery instrument; a two-manual Chancel Organ; and a Kenneth Tickell practice organ of 2008.

The church also owns a Steinway B grand piano and a ring of 12 bells.

A professional quartet of singers leads the musical worship at the weekly Sunday Eucharist.

Ensemble performing at the *Sound Unbound* festival at St Giles Cripplegate
(Photo courtesy of Niki Gorick Photography Ltd)

St Helen's Bishopsgate

Web: https://www.st-helens.org.uk
Twitter: @sthelenschurch

Director of Music: Richard Simpkin

This church, originally a Benedictine priory, was founded in 1210. It is the largest extant parish church in the City of London and has more monuments than any other London church apart from Westminster Abbey.

It survived both the Great Fire and the Blitz, but suffered from IRA bomb damage in the early 1990s.

The scientist Robert Hooke is buried here.
The organ, originally built in 1744, was restored several times, including by Hill, Norman & Beard, and then by Goetze & Gwynn in 1996. It is Grade II*-listed.

St James Garlickhythe

Web: https://stjamesgarlickhythe.org
Twitter: @Garlickhythe

Organist: Alderman, Sir Andrew Parmley

A church has stood on the site since the 12th century. It is a stop for pilgrims on the way to Santiago de Compostela, with both places named after St James.

'Garlickhythe' refers to a nearby place where garlic was sold. Following destruction in the Great Fire of London, the current church was built by Sir Christopher Wren and completed in 1682, and is nicknamed 'Wren's Lantern' because of its numerous windows. Eleven Livery Companies use it as their official church.

The current Honorary Organist, Sir Andrew Parmley, is a distinguished musician and educator: Principal of the Harrodian School; Lord Mayor of London 2016–2017; a Past Master of the Worshipful Company of Musicians (his Mother Company); and Chief Executive of the Royal College of Organists since 2018.

Sir Andrew Parmley and singers enjoying a choir practice at St James Garlickhythe, 2016
(Photo courtesy of Niki Gorick Photography Ltd)

St Katharine Cree

Web: https://stkatharinecree.com
Twitter: @StKathCree

St Katharine Cree Church, in Leadenhall Street, is a Jacobean building of 1633, consecrated by William Laud when he was Bishop of London. The name 'Cree' is likely a corruption of 'Christ Church'. It is now a guild church. The bells, cast from the now-defunct Whitechapel Bell Foundry, are rung from a ground floor ringing chamber.

The church's organ was once played by the composers Purcell and Handel, and some of the 17th-century pipework still exists.

A unique event associated with the church is the *Lion Sermon*, preached annually on 16 October or the nearest weekday. It is held in memory of Sir John Gayer, Lord Mayor of London in 1646, who was accosted by a lion while travelling in the Arabian desert. He prayed to God for deliverance and was left unharmed by the lion. Out of gratitude, Gayer endowed a sermon in perpetuity, in memory of the event. The service features a full choir and organ and is followed by buffet refreshments.

St Lawrence Jewry

Web: https://www.stlawrencejewry.org.uk
Twitter: @StLawrenceJewry

Director of Music: The late Catherine Ennis (1986–2020)

The guild church of St Lawrence Jewry, next to the Guildhall, is the church of the Lord Mayor and the City of London Corporation. It was destroyed in the Great Fire of London and rebuilt by Sir Christopher Wren.

St Lawrence has a vibrant musical tradition, including a longstanding series of Monday lunchtime piano recitals and Tuesday lunchtime organ recitals, together with other concerts through the year, with emphasis on student and prizewinning young musicians within the annual recital programme.

Until her untimely death in late 2020, Catherine Ennis was Director of Music for over 30 years, during which time she oversaw the installation of a new Klais organ in 2001. She was a past President of the Royal College of Organists, holding that office from 2013 to 2015 during the College's 150th anniversary celebrations. She also founded the London Organ Concerts Guide, to promote the organ to a wider audience.

St Lawrence Jewry is the guild church of the City of London Corporation
(Photo courtesy of the late Catherine Ennis, Director of Music at St Lawrence
Jewry)

St Magnus the Martyr

Web: http://www.stmagnusmartyr.org.uk
Twitter: @StMagnusMartyr

Director of Music: William Johnston Davies

The church was designed by Sir Christopher Wren. It is situated on the
crossroads of the old London Bridge at the entry to the City of London.
A model of that old bridge is on display in the church.

The four-manual organ that was built by Abraham Jordan in 1712 was
the first organ in the country to include a swell box. This development

made it possible for a musical phrase to be made louder or softer on the organ, by opening or closing the box, independently from changing the stops that are drawn.

It is the guild church of the Worshipful Company of Fishmongers and the Worshipful Company of Plumbers.

The church offers a weekly Solemn High Mass on Sunday, sung by a small choir of professional singers.

A new ring of 12 bells was installed in 2009.

St Margaret Lothbury

Web: http://stml.org.uk
Twitter: @StMagsLothbury

Organist: Richard Townend

The church has existed since the 12th century. It was rebuilt in 1440 by Robert Large, Lord Mayor under whom William Caxton served his apprenticeship.

The organ was built in 1801 by George Pike England and was once played by Felix Mendelssohn. It was restored in 1984, with its original case and mostly original pipework.

Organ recitals are held on Thursday lunchtimes except in August. Richard Townend has been the resident organist since 1967 and has given over 1000 recitals there.

St Margaret Pattens

Web: http://www.stmargaretpattens.org
Twitter: @MargaretPattens

Director of Music: Rupert Perkins (since 1997)

The current church of St Margaret Pattens was built by Wren and survived largely unscathed from the Second World War.

The church's name, St Margaret Pattens, refers to 'pattens', wooden-soled shoes that worshippers were asked to remove on entering the church. The church is now the guild church of the Worshipful Company of Pattenmakers.

The first documentary reference to an organ at the church is from 1516. In 1749, the present organ, with an elaborately carved case, was built or provided by Thomas Griffin, who was later Gresham Professor of Music. An appeal is currently underway for the restoration of the organ.

The church currently holds a monthly weekday lunchtime choral communion service, with choir members including City office workers.

St Martin Ludgate (or St Martin within Ludgate)

Web: http://www.stmartin-within-ludgate.org.uk
Twitter: @StMartinLudgate

This Wren church provides an oasis of calm on Ludgate Hill, close to the west end of St Paul's Cathedral.

It is a guild church, now under the operational control of the Stationers' Company.

The church has a Bechstein grand piano and a Theodore Bates organ of 1848. The church holds lunchtime music recitals on Mondays from 1:05 – 2 PM for most of the year.

St Mary Abchurch

Web: https://www.achurchnearyou.com/church/15387

Organist: Ian Shaw (since 1995)

The church holds a weekly lunchtime organ recital on Tuesdays, and a Sunday afternoon Eucharist in Russian with singing, guitar and organ.

The Friends of the City Churches, an architectural heritage charity, is based at this church.

St Mary-at-Hill

Web: https://www.stmary-at-hill.org
Twitter: @maryathill

Director of Music: Robert Mingay-Smith

Built in 1336, the church was badly damaged in the Great Fire of London in neighbouring Pudding Lane. Sir Christopher Wren rebuilt the interior. A further fire caused damage in 1988.

In the 16th century, the Chapel Royal choir sang here. Thomas Tallis was organist in 1538–1539.

The historically significant William Hill organ from 1848, damaged in the 1988 fire, was restored by Mander between 2000 and 2002.

The Square Mile Music Series takes place on Tuesday lunchtimes.

St Mary-le-Bow

Web: https://www.stmarylebow.org.uk
Twitter: @BowBellsChurch

Director of Music: Thomas Allery (since 2018)

The current church was built by Sir Christopher Wren following the Great Fire of London.

The bells of Bow are world-famous, and anyone born within their earshot is designated a Cockney. Dick Whittington heard the Bow bells summon him on his return to London to become Lord Mayor in 1392.

The famous nursery rhyme, *Oranges and Lemons*, refers to, among others, "the great bell of Bow". The contemporary composer, Alan Wilson, wrote a toccata for organ that combines the *Oranges and Lemons* tune and a carillon bells chime based on a tune by Charles Villiers Stanford.

The church has two organs: a west gallery Kenneth Tickell organ and a smaller chamber organ. The main organ has a case and reed stops of French character, while also having a Germanic pleno ('full') organ registration suited to the music of J.S. Bach and his contemporaries.

Since 2016, the Academy of St Mary-le-Bow provides opportunities for young orchestral musicians to perform to a high standard, here and elsewhere in London.

In 2019, the Cheapside Chorus was set up for singers who live and work in the City.

St Mary le Strand

Web: https://stmarylestrand.com
Twitter: @StMaryLeStran10

Director of Music: Nigel Groome

This church was built to a Baroque design by James Gibbs in 1724. Together with St Clement Danes, it is an island church on the Strand, and the two churches are in a united parish.

It is the official church of the Women's Royal Naval Service (the Wrens), which holds an annual carol service here.

The church has a weekly Wednesday evening Sung Eucharist, and occasionally Choral Evensong on a Sunday.

St Mary Moorfields

Web: http://www.stmarymoorfields.net/index.php

This Roman Catholic church near Moorgate counts Vincent Novello among its former organists. The current organ is located in a west-end gallery.

St Mary Woolnoth

Web: http://stml.org.uk
Twitter: @stmarywoolnoth1

This church has a west-end gallery organ, rehoused in its 1680s Bernard Smith case by Hill in 1913, who also provided another organ at the east end of the north aisle.

A previous Rector of this church is the famous reformed slave trader, John Newton, who penned the words to the hymn *Amazing Grace*.

St Michael Cornhill

Web: https://www.achurchnearyou.com/church/15372
Twitter: @_stmichaels_

Director of Music: Jonathan Rennert (since 1979)

The church of St Michael's, Cornhill has been renowned for its musical excellence since at least 1375, when its choir of boys and professional singers together with chantry priests sang three services daily, praying at the chantry altars for the soul of the altar's donor, a common practice in churches of pre-Reformation England.

In 1684, after the Great Fire of London in 1666, a Renatus Harris organ was installed. John Blow was invited with "other eminent Musick Masters [who included Henry Purcell] to a Dinner and to try the Organ".

In the 18th century, Cornhill was no stranger to child prodigy musicians, with the young brothers Charles and Samuel Wesley being given free keyboard tuition by the St Michael's organist, William Boyce, while William Crotch gave an organ recital for King George III at the age of three and a half. At the Swan and Hoop, Cornhill, there were daily performances by "… the greatest Prodigy that Europe, or that even Human Nature has to boast of … the little German Boy WOLFGANG MOZART".

Samuel Green was an organ builder who oversaw the rebuilding of the St Michael's organ in 1790. Richard Stevens (organist of St Michael's, 1781–1810) was responsible for identifying the composer of the music of what later became the United States of America's national anthem. That music, composed by John Stafford Smith, organist of the Chapel Royal, was initially sung by amateur musicians after supper at the Crown and

Anchor Tavern in the Strand, to the words of *To Anacreon in Heaven*. The tune was later paired with the words of *The Star-Spangled Banner*.

In the 19th century, St Michael's organist Richard Limpus was the founder of the Royal College of Organists, in 1864. In the FRCO and ARCO examinations – the benchmark of professional achievement for British organists – the highest-scoring candidates in the performance part are, to this day, awarded the Limpus Prize.

In the 20th century, St Michael's was fortunate to have the services of renowned organist and choir trainer Dr Harold Darke for half a century, from 1916 to 1966. He soon recruited a voluntary choir, the St Michael's Singers, who gave annual free performances, in English, of Bach's St John Passion and Christmas Oratorio, together with the B minor Mass and contemporary English music. Ralph Vaughan Williams became the Singers' President, and was succeeded by Herbert Howells. Darke gave over 1800 lunchtime organ recitals at St Michael's during his tenure, and several more during retirement. He is best known as a composer for the choral setting of the Christmas carol, In the Bleak Midwinter, together with Anglican service settings, hymn tunes (one named Cornhill), and a grace composed for the Guild of Air Pilots & Air Navigators. The organ was restored by Nicholson in 2010.
St Michael's has the world's longest-running weekly organ recital series, begun in 1914, every Monday at 1 – 1:50 PM except August and public holidays, with free admission and a retiring collection. These recitals continued online during the COVID-19 lockdowns of 2020–2021.

The professional church choir's latest recording (*Cornhill Visions*, REGCD 550) is a fascinating compilation of just a few of the many choral works which, in the past hundred years, have been composed to be performed in this building, with its resonant acoustic and its superb organ (last restored in 2010). Music by Vaughan Williams and Darke is heard alongside pieces by the current Composer in Residence, Rhiannon Randle. One of her anthems is accompanied by the ethereal sounds of the Chinese stringed instrument, the erhu.

St Michael Paternoster Royal

Web: http://www.london-city-churches.org.uk/Churches/
StMichaelPaternosterRoyal/index.html

The medieval church was rebuilt by Sir Christopher Wren following the Great Fire of London, and again after the Blitz.

London's famed Lord Mayor, Dick Whittington, was buried on the site in 1423, although his remains are now lost.

Since 1968, the church has served as the headquarters of the Mission to Seafarers.

The office of the Bishop of London is now based here.

The church has a Noel Mander organ, housed in a mid-18th-century organ case that is a replica of one from the now-defunct All-Hallows-the-Great church.

The church acoustics are conducive to choral and other musical concert performances.

St Nicholas, Cole Abbey

Web: https://www.stnickschurch.org.uk

The church is named after St Nicholas of Myra, patron saint of children and fishermen, among others, and the church has close links with both groups. The name 'Cole Abbey' derives from 'coldharbour', a shelter from the cold.

In the 1890s, the church attracted as many as 450 worshippers on a Sunday evening. The church was damaged by bombing in 1940 and was rebuilt in 1962. In 1968, it was used as a location in *Doctor Who*.

The church is now the home of the St Nicholas Cole Abbey Centre for Workplace Ministry.

An organ by Bunting was installed in 1824. A new organ by Speechly was built in 1881 and was enlarged in 1931. The current organ, in the reconstructed church, was built by Mander.

St Olave, Hart Street

Web: https://saintolave.com
Twitter: @StOlaveHartSt

Director of Music: Colin Spinks

This church is named after King Olaf II, patron saint of Norway. It was unusual among medieval City churches in surviving the Great Fire of London intact, saved by a combination of the intervention of Sir William Penn (father of the Pennsylvania founder) and a change of wind direction while the flames were burning. It is the burial place of Samuel Pepys.

An organ was built by Samuel Green in 1781. Organists of that time included Mary Hudson, a composer of hymn tunes including possibly *Llandaff*, which is assigned to both her and to her father.

Following the destruction of this organ in the Blitz, a replacement was built by Harrison & Harrison.

Lunchtime recitals take place on Wednesdays and Thursdays.

St Peter ad Vincula, Tower of London

Web: https://www.thechapelsroyalhmtoweroflondon.org.uk
Twitter: @TowerOfLondon

Master of Music: Colm Carey

The church is the parish church of the Tower of London, sited within the Tower's Inner Ward. Many famous prisoners executed at the Tower are buried here, including Sir Thomas More, and the queens Anne Boleyn, Catherine Howard, and Lady Jane Grey..

The current building dates from 1520, and celebrated its 500th anniversary in 2020.

The church is part of the Chapel Royal. That term does not refer to a building, but rather to an establishment of priests and musicians who, since at least the 11th century, would travel with the Sovereign for spiritual ministry. Some of the country's greatest musicians belonged to the Chapel Royal, including, in the first Elizabethan reign, the composers William Byrd and Thomas Tallis. In the 17th century especially, the Chapel Royal was closely associated with Westminster Abbey, and most of the Abbey choir were also Gentlemen of the Chapel Royal. Until the late 17th century, the Master of the Children of the Chapel Royal had the power to bring in young choristers from choirs elsewhere, to sing in the chapel and also perform in court plays with the affiliated theatre company.

The current choral foundation, with a professional Master of Music, organist and choir (today of 12 professional singers), dates from 1965. The first Master of Music was John Williams, formerly an assistant to Herbert Howells, who was in post until 1988. The choir gave recitals and broadcasts, and performed many times in the City of London Festival.

The church previously had a Bernard Smith organ of 1699. It was once played by Handel, and was originally in the Banqueting House, Whitehall. The organ was subsequently enlarged and rebuilt by Hill in the 19th century. In the 1990s, a new organ was commissioned from Létourneau of Quebec, Canada.

Today, the church holds a regular Sunday morning service that is open to the public. As well as singing liturgically for services, the choir also tours, gives concerts, and makes recordings.

St Peter-upon-Cornhill

Web: https://stpeteruponcornhill.org.uk

The church, which was rebuilt by Wren after the Great Fire of London, is built on the highest point in the City of London.

A Smith organ of 1681 was replaced by a Hill organ in 1840. This was during the time that Elizabeth Mounsey was organist. She became organist in 1834 aged 14 and held the position for 48 years. The organ contains an autographed excerpt of the Passacaglia in C minor by J.S. Bach, which Mendelssohn gifted to Mounsey in 1840 following an impromptu performance he gave on the organ at the church.

St Sepulchre without Newgate (or Holy Sepulchre, London)

Web: https://hsl.church

Director of Music: Peter Asprey

This church was rededicated during the Crusades to refer to the Church of the Holy Sepulchre in Jerusalem. It is featured in the nursery rhyme,

Oranges and Lemons, as the "bells of Old Bailey". A handbell was formerly rung every time a prisoner was executed at the nearby Newgate Prison.

In the north aisle is the Musicians' Chapel, dedicated in 1955, which houses the interred ashes of the conductor Sir Henry Wood, the founder of the BBC Promenade Concerts (the Proms). He learned to play the organ here and became assistant organist at age 14. Windows commemorate Sir Henry Wood, the composer John Ireland, the operatic soprano Dame Nellie Melba, and the composer and author Walter Carroll. The Friends of the Musicians' Chapel look after both the Chapel and the Musicians' Book of Remembrance. Those named in the latter book are commemorated in an annual Thanksgiving service and a Requiem service.

St Stephen Walbrook

Web: https://ststephenwalbrook.net
Twitter: @StStephenEC4N

Director of Music: Tom Shorter

The church of St Stephen Walbrook is located close to Mansion House. The present building was constructed by Sir Christopher Wren following the Great Fire of London.

The original church had a memorial to the renowned 15th-century English composer of polyphonic music, John Dunstaple (or Dunstable).

The Samaritans charity was founded in 1953 by the church's rector, Chad Varah. He held the post for 50 years, and at his retirement in 2003, aged 92, he was the oldest serving Church of England minister.

Unusually, the altar is placed in the centre of the church; it is made of white polished stone and was commissioned from the sculptor Henry Moore in 1987. The church has a circular seating layout.

The church has a community choir, which rehearses on Wednesday lunchtimes and leads the worship at a monthly service of Choral Evensong.

Uniquely in the City of London, a 30-minute programme of *Choral Classics* takes place on Monday lunchtimes, sung by the Choral Scholars of St Martin-in-the-Fields and sponsored by the Worshipful Company of Grocers.

The church also hosts regular Tuesday lunchtime music recitals, organised by the Walbrook Music Trust; free Friday lunchtime organ recitals; and monthly music recitals, known as The Lord Mayor's St Stephen Serenades, on a late Friday afternoon with various performers.

Other organisations, such as City of London Livery Companies, organise services here.

St Vedast alias Foster

Web: https://www.vedast.org.uk
Twitter: @StVedast

Director of Music: Joseph Ramadan

The church's original organ was built in 1731 by Renatus Harris for the nearby now-defunct church of St Bartholomew by the Exchange, now the site of an extension to the Bank of England. The organ was restored by the noted organ builder, Noel Mander, who was also a churchwarden at St Vedast at one time.

Today, in addition to Sunday and other services, the church hosts concerts, and various choirs rehearse there.

City organisations that support music

Beyond the many organisations that perform music in the City, there are others whose role is found in support to education, public access, training, examination and awarding in the field of the performing arts.

Note: It has not been possible to include the numerous corporate social responsibility programmes operated by commercial businesses within the Square Mile in partnership with charities that support musical performance in various ways.

Associated Board of the Royal Schools of Music

Web: https://gb.abrsm.org
Twitter: @ABRSM

Founded in 1889, ABRSM moved into offices in the hall of the Worshipful Company of Salters in 2015. This charitable organisation is the examination and awarding body for the four Royal Schools of Music.

ABRSM administers 650,000 exams in 93 countries every year and is also recognised as a centre of excellence for teacher training in music. ABRSM also operates an international sponsorship fund for the teaching of music outside the UK and Ireland.

Barbican Music Library

Web: https://www.cityoflondon.gov.uk/services/libraries-and-archives/our-libraries/Pages/Barbican-Library.aspx
Twitter: @BarbicanMusic

Although part of the Barbican complex, the Music Library warrants separate exploration. Aside from having the largest CD collection of any library in London, the Barbican Music Library also has an online song index of sheet music covering a wide range of genres. The library also offers two electronic pianos, orchestral sets for hire, and listening booths. It runs regular events and exhibitions on aspects of musical history, such as *Tangerine Dream: Zeitraffer* which explored the work of the ground-breaking German electronic music group formed in 1967.

The library is open Monday to Saturday and is located on level 2 in the Barbican Centre. Further details via the Barbican website.

Did you know? The Barbican Music Library also hosts the reference library of the Gilbert and Sullivan Society.

The Worshipful Company of Musicians

Web: https://www.wcom.org.uk
Twitter: @MusiciansComp

The Musicians' Company is the only City of London Livery Company[3] representing the performing arts. The Company traces its origins back to 1500 when it was granted the right to regulate musicians within the City of London, and formed originally in 1350 as the Ancient Society of Minstrels. The Company's arms feature Apollo's swan, the crest is Apollo's lyre, and the Company's motto is 'PRESERVE HARMONY'. Several Past Master Musicians have served as Lord Mayor of London (see appendices).

---

[3] A Livery Company is an occupational guild in the City of London. There are over 100 such Livery Companies representing trades, crafts and professions as diverse as Arbitrators to Wax Chandlers. Originally, the Livery Companies had important roles in regulation of trade, in education and in standards. Today the Livery Companies are also charitable bodies and sponsors of the arts, including music.

The Company is active in many fields of music, including classical, jazz, pop, brass band, and military schools' music. The Company provides support to young musical talent through its annual programme of scholarships, medals and awards, including 'The Prince's Prize', named after HRH Prince Charles, an Honorary Freeman of the Company. The Company is unique in operating a Yeoman Young Artists' Programme that supports young award winners in the early years of their career with publicity, professional development, and five years of performance opportunities.

Two funds, the Maisie Lewis Young Artists' Fund and the Concordia Foundation Artists' Fund, support the debut public recitals of these young musicians. These Yeomen artists also support the Company's Outreach programme, by giving live demonstrations and performances to inner-city primary school children who might not otherwise have an opportunity to see and hear live music. In 2018–2019, the Company organised some 100 visits to over 30 schools, reaching 4,000 children.

In 2020, during the COVID-19 outbreak, the Yeomen artists continued their programme online by using Zoom technology, performing music for SEND pupils (those with special educational needs or disabilities) and people living with Alzheimer's disease and other types of dementia. The artists have also performed in a *Midday Music Young Artists'* Programme, a concert series on the Company's YouTube channel.

Note: The word 'Yeoman' is used for different purposes by other Livery Companies and is usually a grade of membership between Freeman and Liveryman.

Other Livery Companies that support music

The following Livery Companies award prizes, scholarships, bursaries or support musical talent and performance in various ways:

The Worshipful Company of Armourers & Brasiers

The Armourers & Brasiers' Company runs an annual Brass Prize with the Guildhall School of Music and Drama. The prize is awarded to the best soloist.

The Worshipful Company of Brewers

The Brewers' Company is a Trustee of the Dame Alice Owen Foundation (DAOF), which funds the Islington part of Music in Secondary Schools Trust (MiSST) – also supported by the Andrew Lloyd Webber Foundation and the Charles Wolfson Charitable Trust.

MiSST helps secondary schools that have a disadvantaged and challenging student intake by providing not only funding for classical instruments, but also support in the form of regular tuition, opportunities to perform, and a programme of excellence that is unrivalled in the UK.

The DAOF provides funding for Music Education Islington working with the Guildhall School of Music and Drama. The Foundation also provides funding for Dame Alice Owen School and its outstanding music provision. Approximately four hundred pupils receive instrumental lessons. Several pupils attend the junior Saturday morning schools at the Guildhall School of Music, the Royal College of Music and the Royal Academy of Music.

The Worshipful Company of Carmen

The Carmen's Company is one of several that support a chorister at St Paul's Cathedral choir school.

The Worshipful Company of Cordwainers

The Cordwainers' Company supports a number of music projects through charitable giving, including:

City University – Two music scholarships
Guildhall School of Music and Drama – One music scholarship
Guildhall School of Music and Drama – A music outreach project at the Royal Free Hospital
Guildhall School of Music and Drama – A music outreach project at The Urswick School
Royal Society for Blind Children (RSBC) – Support to its music group

The Worshipful Company of Drapers

Throughout its spectacularly long history, the Drapers' Company has supported music, whether performed within its beautiful Hall on the site of Cromwell's palace in the City, or as part of City pageantry for which there is a wealth of detail in the Company's archives especially up to the 17th century.

The Drapers' Company has been associated with St Paul's Cathedral School, London, since the 1960s and makes a grant each year for a bursary for a Drapers' Chorister, who is nominated by the school. The Company also provides support for music education at the Company's affiliated schools and conservatoires.

The Company supports a post-graduate student and, through the Baroness de Turckheim Fund of which the Company is Trustee, a student studying on the prestigious opera programme, or equivalent, at the Royal College of Music; the Royal Academy of Music; the Guildhall School of Music; Trinity Laban Conservatoire of Music and Dance; and the Royal Northern College of Music.

Sir Nicholas Jackson Bt, Master Draper in 1985, is a professional organist and a Liveryman of the Musicians' Company. He was organist of St Lawrence Jewry and St James, Piccadilly in the 1970s.

The Worshipful Company of Needlemakers

The Needlemakers' Company presents an annual Needlemakers' Woodwind Prize with the Guildhall School of Music and Drama. The prize will be presented for the 29th year in 2021.

The Worshipful Company of Parish Clerks

The Parish Clerks' Company sponsors a choir boy at St Paul's Cathedral School with a music bursary to help with fees as they all play two instruments. It also supports the choirs of St Paul's Cathedral and Southwark Cathedral as well as the Friends of Cathedral Music.

The Worshipful Company of Turners

The Turners' Company has long links with the tradition of music making going back to 1604, when both the Turners' Company and the Worshipful Company of Musicians received their Royal Charters. Over the following 150 years of the Baroque period, Masters of the Turners' Company included leading makers such as William Shaw (1635), William Whitehill (1687), and Thomas Stanesby Junior (1739). In the Classical period (1750–1830) Richard Potter created the famous Potter Flute and was Master of the Company in 1782.

The Turners' Consort
(Photo courtesy of the Turners' Company)

Commissioned in 2018 by the Worshipful Company of Turners from Tim Cranmore, one of the UK's leading instrument makers, and curated by Professor Ian Wilson of the Guildhall School of Music & Drama (based in the heart of the City of London), the Turners' Consort is the first set of medieval-style, wood-turned instruments to be played and used for teaching at a UK conservatoire, offering a unique resource for students of woodwind and historical performance.

The Turners' Consort comprises eight instruments in two different keys, to maximise the repertoire that can be played. The instruments are made from European pear wood giving the Consort a warm sound.

City Music Society

Web: https://www.citymusicsociety.org

City Music Society was founded in 1943 by Ivan Sutton MBE, a City tea merchant, and Edric Cundell, principal of the Guildhall School of Music and Drama. The Society was inspired by concerts given by Dame Myra Hess during the early years of the Second World War at the National Gallery and the Royal Exchange. Initially, City Music Society performed concerts in Goldsmiths' Hall and latterly in the Bishopsgate Institute. The former Free Winter Series of concerts was ended in 2017 following the demise of the City of London Festival.

Today, City Music Society performs regular lunchtime and evening concerts which are held in the Priory Church of St Bartholomew the Great (Smithfield) and the Guildhall School of Music and Drama. While the Society's concerts are open to the public, and lunchtime concerts are free to attend, the Society is a membership organisation with ordinary membership starting at £15 (2021 prices). Membership supports the work of the Society and members receive a discount off the ticket price for those evening concerts where an entry fee is charged.

City Music Society receives support from the Worshipful Company of Musicians for its annual Spring Concert Series and, additionally, from the Eric Falk Trust and Royal Philharmonic Society for individual concerts.

City Music Foundation

Web: http://www.citymusicfoundation.org
Twitter: @CityMusicF

This is a relatively new organisation for the City of London. City Music Foundation (CMF) was founded in 2012 and has counted among its trustees two past Lord Mayors of London who have also served as Master of the Musicians' Company: The late Sir Roger Gifford (founder) and Sir Andrew Parmley. In addition, Sir Nicholas Kenyon and Kathryn McDowell are on the Board. CMF exists to turn exceptional musical talent into lasting professional success by providing emerging musicians with a range of career development initiatives and management. Artists are selected through an annual series of auditions judged by an independent panel of music industry leaders. Successful applicants are supported over a two-year period with a programme of mentoring and performance that blends the development of business skills with artistic talent. CMF further enables artists by acting as their agent for commercial bookings.

In 2019, City Music Foundation joined forces with the City's Culture Mile to provide musical performances at venues along the route including the rather unusual venue of St Bartholomew's Hospital Pathology Museum. CMF also supports musical talent and the local community by putting on regular lunchtime concerts in the Hospital Church of St Bartholomew the Less.

During the COVID-19 lockdown in 2020, City Music Foundation organised a series of online concerts by their artists, broadcast live without an audience, from St Pancras Clock Tower. In October 2020, they performed Olivier Messiaen's *Quartet for the End of Time* at St Paul's Cathedral, to a socially distanced audience of 300 people. In 2021, City Music Foundation curated a series of lunchtime concerts broadcast live online, as well as with an in-person audience, from the historic setting of the Great Hall of St Bartholomew's Hospital.

CMF artists in the Great Hall of St Bartholomew's Hospital
(Photo courtesy of Clare Taylor)

Applications for the annual auditions are welcomed via the CMF website during early spring. A selection of videos of current and past artists and events may also be viewed on the website.

Temple Music Foundation

Web: https://www.templemusic.org
Twitter: @templemusicfdn

In June 2003, *The Veil of the Temple*, an epic all-night vigil commissioned from Sir John Tavener, was performed at the Temple Church without a break during the seven hours between dusk and dawn. The Temple Music Foundation (TMF) was established to present *The Veil of the Temple.*

Since then, TMF has promoted an annual programme of around 20 events a year in the Temple's three venues: the Elizabethan Middle Temple Hall, Inner Temple's Parliament Chamber, and the 12th-century Temple Church. The repertoire is a mixture of choral, orchestral and chamber music, and includes the Temple Song series of solo recitals curated by pianist Julius Drake. The TMF works particularly closely with the Temple Church Choir, which gives a regular series of concerts throughout the year as part of the TMF programme.

In addition to intimate recitals, some of the Temple Music Foundation events have been on a large scale and have commemorated major anniversaries. In 2016, to mark the 400th anniversary of the death of Shakespeare, a staged performance of *A Midsummer Night's Dream* took place in Middle Temple Hall, interspersed with Mendelssohn's incidental music of the same title. Later in 2016, to commemorate the 350th anniversary of the Great Fire of London in 1666, a specially commissioned opera, *And London Burned*, by the contemporary composer Matt Rogers was performed in the Temple Church. Both of these events were followed by a gala dinner in Inner Temple Hall.

During the COVID-19 pandemic of 2020–2021, Temple Music Foundation launched Temple Music at Home, a regular series of short, online musical performances.

The Temple Music Foundation sells a range of choral and organ CDs and music-related books via its website.

See also 'Temple Church'.

A concert in the Temple Church
(Photo courtesy of the Temple Music Foundation)

Guildhall School of Music and Drama

Web: https://www.gsmd.ac.uk
Twitter: @guildhallschool

Founded in 1880 with fees initially set at one guinea per term, this independent school is funded by the City of London Corporation, and is one of three private schools for which the City is responsible. The school has a global reputation for the excellence of its teaching and has produced a long line of leading figures in the world of music and acting. To name but a few among many luminaries in the performing arts, the following are graduates from the school: Honor Blackman, Daniel Craig, James Galway, Myleene Klass and Damian Lewis.

The Guildhall School of Music and Drama is an institution of international importance located within the Barbican complex
(Photo © Paul D Jagger)

In 1915, Sir Henry Dixon Kimber Bt, sometime Chief Commoner, provided funds for an annual award: the Guildhall School Gold Medal. Since 1950, the medal has been awarded to a singer one year and an instrumentalist the next. Past winners include, among others:

- Sir Bryn Terfel CBE
- Max Jaffa OBE
- Tasmin Little OBE
- Jacqueline du Pré OBE

In addition to the school's regular teaching programme, it runs a series of short courses during the summer months and during weekday evenings throughout the year on acting, the history of music, public speaking, and other allied topics.

Note: Guildhall School of Music and Drama developed from an earlier Guildhall Orchestral Society founded in 1878. Its first director was Mr Weist Hill who was renowned at the time as the greatest living English conductor and an accomplished violinist. The Secretary of the Guildhall Orchestral Society was Mr Charles Smith. Both Hill and Smith went on to become, respectively, founding Director and Secretary of the Guildhall School of Music and Drama.

Centre for Young Musicians

Web: https://cym.org.uk
Twitter: @CYMLondon and @LYWBlondon

The Centre for Young Musicians (CYM) describes itself as a "division of the Guildhall School of Music and Drama" and celebrated its 50th anniversary in 2020. It has branches in London, Norwich, Taunton, Saffron Walden, and Peterborough. CYM also manages the London Schools Symphony Orchestra, sponsored by the City of London Corporation, and the London Youth Wind Band.

CYM is supported by the Foundation for Young Musicians and the Friends of the Centre for Young Musicians – a network of parents and relatives of current CYM pupils and alumni. CYM is focused on providing training in an inclusive, vibrant and stimulating environment through its Saturday centre and summer schools.

Song in the City

Web: https://www.songinthecity.org
Twitter: @SongintheCity

This charity uses the power of song to improve lives. Song in the City runs a regular series of projects that are designed to address matters of well-being. An example is *Creative Madness in Song*, in which young composers from the Guildhall School of Music and Drama create new songs from poems written by users of mental health services. Another is *Healthy Lunchbreaks*, which has delivered over 150 free lunchtime performances. The performances are typically held in church venues around the City and surrounding boroughs.

In 2012, Song in the City commissioned a song-cycle titled *Voices of London* which comprised songs by four composers and four singers from the Guildhall School of Music.

City University, London (Department of Music)

Web: https://www.city.ac.uk/about/schools/arts-social-sciences/
music
Twitter: @CityUniLondon

City University, London opened its music department in 1975 and by 2019 it was ranked 15th among music schools in the UK. The department has a strong heritage in technology, electronic and electro-acoustic music; it offers a range of performance scholarships for undergraduate study of music.

City University is home to SPARC (Sound Practice and Research at City), an independent research centre which hosts, among many other one-off events, an annual SPARCfest exploring aspects of music and sound. SPARC has a wide range of visiting musicians with a particular emphasis on artists engaged in improvisation, and electronic and electro-acoustic music.

Gresham College

Web: https://www.gresham.ac.uk
Twitter: @GreshamCollege

Founded in 1597, Gresham College remains at the heart of the City's commitment to free public education. It runs a regular series of lectures on a wide range of topics, including many that explore the cultural aspects of the City. The College's first Professor of Music, John Bull, was appointed at the recommendation of Queen Elizabeth I and was in post in 1596, a year before the College formally opened.

In 2020, Professor Marina Frolova-Walker, Professor of Music History and Director of Studies in Music at Clare College, Cambridge, became the first female Professor of Music appointed to Gresham College. Professor Frolova-Walker was previously a visiting professor to Gresham College, specialising in Russian music.

A full programme of public lectures, including recordings of past lectures, may be found on Gresham College's website.

The Friends of the City Churches

Web: http://www.london-city-churches.org.uk
Twitter: @ChurchWatchers

This organisation is an architectural heritage charity that supports the City of London churches. The Friends of the City Churches produces a regularly issued *City Events* guide to concerts and other events in the City churches, and produces a map of these churches. It helps with conservation of the churches and brings people together by means of visits, tours and walks to promote the heritage and contemporary life of these churches.

City organisations that perform music

Academy of St Mary-le-Bow

Web: https://www.academyofstmarylebow.com/
Twitter: @acadstmarylebow

The Academy of St Mary-le-Bow, formed in 2016 and directed by Alex Fryer, is a chamber orchestra composed of non-professional musicians who work in London. The orchestra is based at the church of St-Mary-le-Bow and performs several concerts each year.

The Ancient Society of College Youths

Web: http://ascy.org.uk

A misnomer befitting the City's custom of strange titles, the Ancient Society of College Youths is the premier association of bellringers in the Square Mile. The Society was formed in 1637 and rings at St Paul's Cathedral and a number of other major rings in the City and beyond. A peal board in the Curfew Tower of St George's Chapel, Windsor Castle, records an event in 1787 when the College Youths rang a "True and complete peal of 5040 Grandsire Triples in 4 hours and 14 minutes".

The Society has a governance structure similar to a Livery Company and is led by an annually elected Master. Its definition of youth seems quite flexible as the Society maintains an honour roll of active members with 50, 60 or 70 years of membership.

The Society also supports the restoration of church bells in those churches where it has a major interest. To this end, the Society operates a charitable trust known as the Bell Restoration Fund.

A curious membership requirement for this Society is that no member may also be a member of The Society of Royal Cumberland Youths, another bellringing society with its headquarters at St Martin-in-the-Fields, Westminster.

City Bach Collective

Web: http://citybachcollective.org.uk
Twitter: @City_Bach

Formed in early 2016 in the tradition of the City Bach Cantata Series, which celebrated its 40th anniversary in November of that year, the City Bach Collective plays the music of Johann Sebastian Bach and his contemporaries on period instruments. This group of professional musicians, many of whom hail from the Royal Academy of Music, plays the Bach Vespers series in churches in the City of London, particularly in St Anne's Lutheran Church. The City Bach Collective also participates in the annual Bach Festival, which is held in the City every July in St Mary-at-Hill Church.

Did you know? Research has shown that spiders prefer classical music to popular music. In particular, they enjoy Bach and will hasten the building of webs when listening to it.

A concert given by the City Bach Collective
(Photo courtesy of the City of London Bach Collective)

The City Glee Club

Twitter: @CityGleeClub

The City Glee Club lays claim to being the oldest musical club in London. It was founded in 1669 in the wake of the Great Fire of London three years earlier, when many gentlemen singers lost their jobs when churches were destroyed, and they earned an income instead by performing in the inns and hostelries of London.

The Glee Club has counted Aldermen of the City of London, Members of Parliament and Baronets among its members, and the Lord Mayor of London is always the club's Honorary President.

They perform concerts of glees, catches and madrigals, from 140-year-old leather-bound song books. Recent performances have been at the Charterhouse and at St Peter, Hammersmith with a light supper in the interval.

City of London Choir

Web: https://cityoflondonchoir.org
Twitter: @CityLondonChoir

Singing since 1963, the City of London Choir rehearses weekly in the City and draws its energetic membership from the Square Mile and well beyond. The choir has a broad repertoire with a particular reputation for 20th-century English music, and performs with London's leading orchestras at major venues including the Barbican Centre, the Royal Albert Hall, Cadogan Hall, the Royal Festival Hall and St John's Smith Square.

A not-for-profit charity with a particular mission to encourage young singers and audiences, the choir is strictly non-professional and operates to professional standards. Its numerous recordings as well as an archive of past performances and a prospectus of future concerts may be found on the choir's website.

Did you know? In 2017, the City of London Choir recorded an album titled *The Nation's Favourite Christmas Carols* with the Royal Philharmonic Orchestra in association with Classic FM.

The City of London Choir and the Royal Philharmonic Orchestra on stage at the Barbican Hall
(Photo © Roger Way 2016, courtesy of the City of London Choir)

Livery Company Choirs

Several of the City of London Livery Companies have their own choir, including:

- The Worshipful Company of Carmen
- The Worshipful Company of Educators
- The Worshipful Company of Horners
- The Worshipful Company of Salters
- The Worshipful Company of World Traders

Lloyd's Choir

Web: https://www.lloydschoir.com/
Twitter: @LloydsChoir

Director of Music: Jacques Cohen (since 1995)

Lloyd's Choir, formed in 1922, has around 80 singers. Its membership is drawn predominantly from those working in the insurance community of Lloyd's and the London Market. St Katharine Cree Church has been the choir's home for over 50 years and is where it meets to rehearse and gives many of its concerts.

The choir normally gives four concerts each year, including a major orchestral concert in the spring. Repertoire is wide-ranging, from early polyphony to contemporary, including several premieres. The choir is delighted to have performed numerous works written specially for it. In addition, members of the choir sing for church services in the City and have sung Choral Evensong at Canterbury Cathedral. An important commitment in the choir's calendar is the annual Remembrance commemorations in the Underwriting Room at Lloyd's.

Lloyd's Choir welcomes new singers, especially in the lower voice parts. While there are no formal auditions, new members join for a trial period, and the choir performs to a high standard. Rehearsals are normally held on Monday lunchtimes.

Lloyd's Choir in St Giles Cripplegate
(Photo courtesy Lloyd's Choir)

London City Orchestra

Web: https://www.londoncityorchestra.com
Twitter: @LondonCityOrch

A relative newcomer to the City's musical scene, the London City
Orchestra (LCO) was founded in 2013 and has since grown to a full
orchestra that comprises professional musicians, students of music and
amateurs. LCO is a thriving and energetic symphony orchestra based at
St Botolph without Aldersgate. LCO performs several concerts
throughout the year at venues within and outside the Square Mile.

LCO carefully chooses repertoire that inspires listeners of all ages at its engaging concerts. Musical Director Thomas Payne leads the orchestra with a unique style and passion in performances of a high standard.

The LCO supports local charities and musical education in the City; it also operates a Friends scheme and welcomes new members of the orchestra.

London City Voices (Choir)

Web: https://www.londoncityvoices.co.uk
Twitter: @LondonCityVoice

This large, non-audition pop choir meets three times a week in three different locations in central London, including St Mary-at-Hill on Wednesdays.

The brainchild of director Richard Swan, London City Voices (LCV) was launched in 2011 with a handful of members, and has grown to a regular membership of about 400.

Organised on a termly basis, the choir performs a main concert each term in venues such as Troxy and Tobacco Dock; sings at major events including the London Marathon and the Citadel Festival; and takes part in occasional recording projects. Rehearsals are followed by a pub session with much singing and merriment.

LCV regularly raises considerable sums for charity. In December 2019, the choir raised over £14,000 for various charities by singing at major commuter stations, and in 2020 raised over £100,000 for Women's Aid with their lockdown version of Carole King's *You've Got a Friend*. In December 2020, LCV accompanied Annie Lennox on her reworked version of Purcell's *Dido's Lament* to raise money for Greenpeace.

As well as running regular rehearsals, LCV also runs several holidays, including a skiing trip, a summer workshop in Greece, and an autumn weekend away. The choir welcomes singers of all abilities, from novices to professionals. The only requirement is a desire to sing.

London City Voices performing hits from the 1970s
(Photo courtesy of London City Voices)

London City Chorus

Web: http://www.londoncitychorus.com
Twitter: @CityChorusLDN

The City of London Chorus celebrated its 100th anniversary in 2020. The choir's origins are in the company choir of the former National Provincial Bank, which became known as the National Westminster Choir (NatWest) after the merger of the National Provincial and Westminster banks in 1968.

City Chorus meets at St Mary Moorfields, a Roman Catholic church in Moorgate. It prides itself on being a friendly choir that admits all comers without the need for audition.

London Symphony Orchestra

Web: https://lso.co.uk/
Twitter: @londonsymphony

The LSO was founded in 1904, making it the oldest symphony orchestra in London. It has been located at the Barbican Centre since 1982 where it is the resident orchestra. The LSO performs over 120 concerts per year and is recognised as one of the top five orchestras in the world. The Music Director of the LSO is Sir Simon Rattle OM CBE. At his scheduled standing down from the role in 2023, he would become Conductor Emeritus (a title previously held by André Previn KBE), and Sir Antonio Pappano will become Chief Conductor.

Players of the London Symphony Orchestra (LSO) under the watchful eye of their
Music Director, Sir Simon Rattle
(Photo by Mark Allan, courtesy of the LSO)

The orchestra has made more recordings than any other in the world. It has an illustrious history of giving the first performance of notable new works, including Elgar's *Cello Concerto*, Vaughan Williams' *Fantasia on a Theme by Thomas Tallis* and, more recently, Sir James MacMillan's *St John Passion*, among countless others.

The City Musick

Web: https://www.tcmusick.com
Twitter: @TheCityMusick

Styled on the City Waits originally present in London and other cities in the UK, this wind instrument ensemble performs Renaissance-era civic and court music at events in the City of London and elsewhere. In particular, it is known for its role in the Vintners' Company annual Swan Feast.

The City Musick – styled on the ancient City Waits
(Photo courtesy of The City Musick)

City of London Sinfonia

Web: https://cityoflondonsinfonia.co.uk
Twitter: @CityLdnSinfonia

The City of London Sinfonia was founded in 1971 by the conductor
Richard Hickox CBE, who was its Music and Artistic Director until he
passed away in 2008. The City of London Sinfonia is proud of its
"seriously informal style of concert" performance.

St Paul's Cathedral Choirs

Web: https://www.stpauls.co.uk/worship-music/music/cathedral-choirs
Twitter: @StPaulsChoir

St Paul's Cathedral is blessed with no fewer than three choirs and a guild whose membership is made up of former choristers from one of the Cathedral's choirs.

The choristers of St Paul's Cathedral are drawn from the pupils of St Paul's Cathedral School, an independent school which is located adjacent to the Cathedral and was founded in 1123. Formerly, the St Paul's Cathedral Choir Boys School was located on Carter Lane in a building that is now the City's Youth Hostel.

Choristers of St Paul's Cathedral
(Photo © Chapter of St Paul's. Photo by Graham Lacdao.)

Spitalfields Music

Web: https://spitalfieldsmusic.org.uk
Twitter: @SpitsMusic

Spitalfields Music is a music charity that runs a year-round programme of learning and participation work in schools, care homes and community settings, plus concerts and other events, including a summer music festival. The festival uses existing venues and found spaces across the City of London and the East End to plant high-quality musical experiences in the heart of these communities. Additionally, Spitalfields Music runs an industry-leading sector support programme for musicians and composers, supporting emerging talent and providing consultancy support to arts organisations across the UK.

In July 2021, Spitalfields Music Festival welcomed back in-person audiences, featuring 15 world premieres alongside classic repertoire in various East End locations.

Band of the Honourable Artillery Company

Web: https://hac.org.uk
Twitter: @HAC_Band

The Honourable Artillery Company (HAC) is the oldest military unit in the British Armed Forces and the second oldest in the world – only the Vatican Swiss Guard claims greater antiquity. Among the HAC's many facets is the Regimental Band, which is a regular feature of the Lord Mayor's Show and other ceremonial events. The uniform of the band is the same as that of the Grenadier Guards, except that the HAC's uniform is embellished with silver rather than gold on accoutrements such as epaulets.

The HAC also maintains a Corps of Drums, which is a separate sub-unit of the regiment from the band. The HAC's Company of Pikemen and Musketeers also has its 'Musik', which is a Corps of Drums and Fifes which may be seen, dressed in 17th-century uniform, during ceremonial events such as banquets in Mansion House. A wonderful opportunity to watch the HAC's Company of Pikemen and Musketeers march off with their drums and fifes occurs at the very end of the Lord Mayor's Show when the Company salutes the new Lord Mayor at Mansion House before marching back to Armoury House in a journey that takes about 15 minutes. Few people stay to experience this part of the show but it is a fitting finale.

The Band of the Honourable Artillery Company
(Photo courtesy of Colour Sergeant Anthony Johncock, Copyright Honourable Artillery Company)

Lunchbreak Opera

Web: https://www.lunchbreakopera.co.uk
Twitter: @LBOpera

Based in St Botolph's Aldgate, Lunchbreak Opera provides free lunchtime operatic concerts for City workers and tourists. The operatic repertoire is notable for its accessible nature, with performance in English and lasting under an hour. Performances are free to attend, with donations welcome.

Music in Offices

Web: https://musicinoffices.com
Twitter: @MIOLondon

Founded by Tessa Marchington, an alumnus of the Guildhall School of Music and Drama, Music in Offices provides instrumental lessons, choirs, team-building workshops, events (both online and in person), choirs, and concerts all tailored to the needs of the City's business professionals. Music in Offices' activities focus on bringing opportunities for creativity and collaboration through music, forging charity partnerships and bringing the many well-being benefits of participation in the arts to a wider audience.

Music-at-Hill

Web: https://www.facebook.com/MusicAtHill

Describing itself as the friendliest concert society in central London, this concert society was formed in 1969. The society performs regular Friday lunchtime chamber concerts.

Note: The Society recently moved from its former base of St Mary-at-Hill to St Giles-in-the-Fields outside the City of London.

Royal Choral Society

Web: http://www.royalchoralsociety.co.uk
Twitter: @royalchoral

The Royal Choral Society was founded in 1871 to coincide with the opening of the Royal Albert Hall. The Society has its offices on Upper Thames Street in the City of London and regularly performs at City venues such as the Barbican Centre. The Society conducts its rehearsals at the City of London School for Girls within the Barbican Estate.

In 2016, the Society celebrated the 80th birthday of its President, HRH The Duke of Kent, by holding a special invitation-only concert and reception in Westminster Hall. The Masters and consorts of all the City Livery Companies were invited to this special event.

VOCES8 Foundation

Web: https://voces8.foundation
Twitter: @v8_foundation

Formerly known as VCM Foundation, VOCES8 is a vocal charity located at St Anne and St Agnes Church on Gresham Street in what was previously known as the Gresham Centre. VOCES8 was formed in 2005 and specialises in vocal music education. VOCES8 holds an annual season of six concerts and various educational sessions in the City. Events are ticketed and it is possible to purchase a season pass.

In December 2020, with many traditional carol services having to be cancelled because of the COVID-19 pandemic, the VOCES8 group organised instead a *Carols for the City* online service, along with the Lord Mayor's Appeal and the Worshipful Company of Information Technologists.

More than 5000 people watched the service online. VOCES8 themselves were the choir for the service, with an eminent line-up of participants including Alderman William Russell, Lord Mayor (Welcome and Reader); HRH Prince Edward, the Earl of Wessex (Welcome and Reader); Sir Kenneth Olisa, Lord-Lieutenant of Greater London (Reader); Dame Mary Berry DBE (Reader); Dame Sarah Mullally DBE, Bishop of London (Final Blessing); and organists Alderman Sir Andrew Parmley (past Lord Mayor), and Anna Lapwood (Director of Music at Pembroke College, Cambridge).

Summer Music in City Churches

Web: https://www.summermusiccitychurches.com

The newest City concert series, Summer Music in City Churches, began in 2018. The festival endeavours to fill some of the gaps left by the demise of the former City of London Festival by presenting beautiful music in the historic churches of London's Square Mile over ten days in late June. Summer Music in City Churches currently performs in five of the City's churches: St Lawrence Jewry, St Giles Cripplegate, St Mary-le-Bow, St Stephen Walbrook, and St Bride.

Summer Music in City Churches: City of London Choir and London Mozart Players conducted by Hilary Davan Wetton at St Giles Cripplegate
(Photo courtesy of Jenny Robinson and Rosie Robinson)

Other City events and organisations with a musical connection

Presentation of the Cutlers' Company Sword

This ceremony takes place during the annual Lord Mayor's Show and involves the presentation of a sword to the drummer or bugler junior non-commissioned officer of one of the English line regiments who has been identified by the Army's Director of Infantry as having shown exemplary ability and initiative as a musician during that year. As the name suggests, the sword is the gift of the Cutlers' Company and is crafted by Pooley Sword; the Lord Mayor of London presents the sword to the award winner.

The City of London Phonograph and Gramophone Society

Web: https://www.clpgs.org.uk/

This society celebrated its centenary in 2019 and is the oldest society in the world to specialise in the field of recorded sound. It has approximately 600 members worldwide and its objective is to promote education in the art, science and history of the reproduction of sound. It was originally titled The London Edison Society when Thomas Edison, the inventor of the phonograph, became its first patron.

The society promotes original research through an annual bursary scheme and publishes a wide range of reference material and a quarterly magazine *For the Record*. It has held a monthly meeting in central London since 1919, interrupted only by the Second World War and COVID-19 restrictions, and holds regular regional group meetings.

Concerts of original recordings from as early as 1887 can be heard on the Society's website.

MSCTY x Sculpture in the City

Web: https://www.sculptureinthecity.org.uk/whats-on/musicity
Twitter: @sculpturecity

This innovative collaboration between Music City and the Culture Mile brings a musical aspect to some of the landmarks along the Culture Mile. Artists have created 11 musical tracks that one may listen to online with an app for mobile devices, but only when in proximity of the landmark to which they relate.

The landmarks and track names (if not the same as the landmark) are:

- 70 St Mary Axe
- Aldgate Tower
- 99 Bishopsgate (Dulcian Gate)
- Bury Court (Can I sit here)
- Principal Place (London City)
- 1 Undershaft (Full as Deep)
- St Helen's Square (Glass and Steel)
- Lime Street (Inside Out)
- St Botolph without Bishopsgate Churchyard (Show Me)
- Leadenhall Market (£4.80 salmon-roll (bap), £2.50 cup of coffee, £5.50 cheese-cake)
- Mitre Square (A Penny Beautiful for Catherine Eddowes)

Livery Company Anthems, Songs and Themes

The City's Livery Companies probably originated as religious guilds before the Norman Conquest. As the guilds evolved to become occupational Livery Companies, they retained their links with the established church, while admitting members of any faith or none. Some of the Companies have a hymn that is sung at particular services during the year, and most of the Companies are affiliated with a church in the City.

Several of the City's Livery Companies also boast songs that are sung by diners at formal events. These songs usually recall a Company's links with its trade, craft or profession; exalt the membership to celebrate the Company fame; or recall some noble achievement worthy of celebration. Monarchs, charters, fellowship, feasting and drinking are common themes among the songs and, while some are sober and reflective, more often they are jolly and uplifting.

Only the Horners' Company has a song which claims it is the best; we've listed it alphabetically with all the rest ....

A list of the websites of the various City of London Livery Companies and Livery Halls mentioned in this guide may be found in at https://www.liverycommittee.org

The Worshipful Society of Apothecaries

The Apothecaries' Society (the only Livery Company styled 'Society') commissioned an anthem from Michael Berkeley CBE (Baron Berkeley of Knighton) to celebrate the Society's 400th anniversary. The anthem was first performed in 2017 and is a setting of *Heare us, O heare us,*

Lord by John Donne, who was Dean of St Paul's Cathedral from 1621 to 1631:

> *Heare us, O heare us Lord,*
> *To thee a sinner is more music when he prayes,*
> *Than spheares, or Angels praises bee*
> *In Panegerique Alleluias,*
> *O Heare us, for till thou heare us, Lord;*
> *We know not what to say;*
> *Thine eare to our sighes, teares,*
> *Thoughts give voice and word*
> *O Thou who Satan heard in Job's sicke day,*
> *Heare thy selfe now, for thou in us dost pray.*
> *That learning, thine Ambassador,*
> *From thine allegiance we never tempt,*
> *That beauty, paradise's flower*
> *For physicke made, from poison be exempt,*
> *That wit borne apt high good to doe,*
> *By dwelling lazily on Nature's nothing,*
> *Be not nothing too, that our affections kill us not, nor dye,*
> *Heare us, O thou eare, weak echoes, and cry,*
> *Sonne of God heare us, and since thou*
> *By taking our blood owest it us againe*
> *Gaine to thy self, or us allow;*
> *And let not both us and Thy selfe be slaine;*
> *O Lambe of God, which took'st our sinne*
> *Which could not stick to thee,*
> *O let it not return to us againe,*
> *But patient and physition being free,*
> *As sinne is nothing, let it nowhere be.*

The Worshipful Company of Blacksmiths

The Company song dates from 1828 and is sung every year at the Company's principal banquet in Mansion House. The song comprises three verses and a chorus which ends with the Company's motto:

In the good olden days when the gods condescended
To visit this Earth and enlighten mankind,
Amongst those who most us poor mortals befriended,
Still Vulcan, our Patron, the foremost you'll find;
When he taught us with Anvil and Hammer to mould
The Ploughshare, the Spade, and the Sickle to reap,
Had we paid for such knowledge a mountain of gold,
The purchase would still to mankind have been cheap.

To the mem'ry of Vulcan our voices we'll raise,
May he and his sons be revered thro' the land;
May they thrive root and branch, and enjoy happy days
For by Hammer and Hand all arts do stand.

Withdraw the utensils produced by our art,
And with them the best comforts of life will retreat;
Without Knives or Forks we should look mighty smart;
As with unshaven chins we sat gnawing our meat.
Withdraw but the Axe and the Saw, and the Plane,
Not a Table or Chair would be made for our use;
To the mud-hut we would soon be driven again –
The best, without us, that man's art could produce.

To the mem'ry of Vulcan our voices we'll raise,
May he and his sons be revered thro' the land;
May they thrive root and branch, and enjoy happy days
For by Hammer and Hand all arts do stand.

Still duly devoted to Love and to Beauty,
Each true Son of Vulcan will ever be found;
For Venus herself taught our Grandsire this duty,
And with all her sweet charms she his gallantry crown'd.

And still ev'ry lovely young Maiden will prove
To Vulcan's descendants most yielding and kind;
For the good Man of Metal, in matters of love,
Has always the highest regard in her mind.

To the mem'ry of Vulcan our voices we'll raise,
May he and his sons be revered thro' the land;
May they thrive root and branch, and enjoy happy days
For by Hammer and Hand all arts do stand.

The Worshipful Company of Bowyers

The Bowyers' Company has several unique characteristics for a Livery Company: it is the only Company that elects a Master for a two-year term of office and it is the only one that toasts a past benefactor without speaking his name.

The Bowyers' Song is a 19th- century curiosity. Its dedication page attributes it to "S Sangster Past Master" 1834–1836. A Court minute of 1848 records that "the Court requested Mr Samuel Sangster to perpetuate his song called *The Bowyers' Song* which he had composed and had sung on Visitors' Day" (the Autumn Dinner). In January 1849, Mr Sangster presented the Company with the printing plates and 50 copies.

It is not known how long the practice continued, and it eventually fell into disuse. The words and the music were rediscovered and reintroduced by Clive Arding, Master 2002–2004.

The Bowyers' Song features four verses and four choruses that extol the virtues of the English Bowman and his achievements in battle at Agincourt, Poitiers and Crécy. The song is now sung with gusto at all the Bowyers' October Agincourt Dinners. The lyrics are included here with the kind permission of the Company:

While seated together so social and free,
My bold brother Bowyers around me I see;
What theme should inspire, What strain rather flow,
Than a song in the praise of our Old English Bow.
Our firm sinew'd Bowmen in ages long past,
Gain'd that fame by their courage that ever will last,
They protected their rights by the strength of their Bow,
While their wrongs they aveng'd upon each daring foe;
While their wrongs they aveng'd upon each daring foe;

Chorus
And still Agincourt, Poitiers, Cressy, can tell
What thousands of Frenchmen by Brave Bowyers fell.
What thousands of Frenchmen by Brave Bowyers fell.

Through the Bow now less used to the Musket gives place,
With either we'll still meet our foes face to face,
In support of our Country our Children our Wives,
The Bowyers wou'd hazard their Fortune their Lives,
And tho' these same Frenchmen have always been known,
To shoot with a monst'rous Long Bow of their own,
Shou'd they Coward like trusting to darkness and flight,
Escape our brave Tars midst of Fogs or by Night;
Escape our brave Tars midst of Fogs or by night;

Chorus
And shou'd e 'er touch our Coast to their cost they will know,
That Englishmen still have two Strings to their Bow.
That Englishmen still have two Strings to their Bow.

In the Joys of the Chase, what cou'd bring down a Doe,
Or our Grandsires please like an old British Bow,
Such Exercise thus, Health and Strength always yield,
And no pleasure they priz'd like the Joys of the Field.
Little Cupid we know, cou'd not e'en kill a Sparrow,
Depriv'd of his Bow, of his Quiver, his Arrow,
But with these he commands all the Hearts of the Fair,
And Conquers by Love, and subdues ev'ry Care.
And Conquers by Love, and subdues ev'ry Care.

Chorus
May our Love and esteem for the Bow never cease,
That gives Safety in War, Health and Pleasure in Peace.
That gives Safety in War, Health and Pleasure in Peace.

Though the merit they claim, chiefly lays in their Bow,
Place a Fine Haunch before 'em they'll presently shew
At a good Knife and Fork they are not to be Beat,
But can play well their part, while there's plenty to Eat;
Then a Glass of good Liquor, and give it good measure,
To the Bowyers the Lads of true Courage and Pleasure,
Whose Glass is his Arrow, whose Bottle's his Bow,
Whose Aim is good Humour, dull Care is the Foe.
Whose Aim is good Humour, dull Care is the Foe.

Chorus
Whose Heart is his Sov'reign's, whose Laws he defends,
Whose Blood is his Country's, whose Bottle's his Friends.
Whose Blood is his Country's, whose Bottle's his Friends.

The Worshipful Company of Brewers

The Brewers' Company has a song which, perhaps apt for its trade, is known as a glee, and the words indicate a certain jollity that may be attributed to more than one glass of the Brewers' ale as the chorus suggests. The origins of the glee are unclear but first appear among the songs listed in the Company's election dinner of 1884.

'Tis Merry, 'Tis Merry in Brewers Hall.
While the welcome cup goes round,
When assembled here at the Master's call,
Good humour and mirth abound.

Then fill the glass to our standing toast,
No divisions our unions shall sever,
May the Brewers' Company root and branch,
In Prosperity, flourish for ever.

For here in years that have long since past,
The tie of fellow ship bound us,
And here old time as he Journeys along,
In Harmony still has found us.

Then fill the glass to our standing toast,
No divisions our unions shall sever,
May the Brewers Company root and branch,
In Prosperity, flourish for ever.

Our flowing cups to the Master's health,
A-round shall cheerily pass,
The song and the glee to enliven our board,
Shall join with the circling glass.

Then fill the glass to our standing toast,
No divisions our unions shall sever,
May the Brewers' Company root and branch,
In Prosperity, flourish for ever.

The Worshipful Company of Broderers

The Worshipful Company of Broderers (Embroiderers) maintains the tradition of the Master's Song which, as its title suggests, is sung by the Master at formal banquets. It has become a point of honour that the song should be sung out of tune, and the worse the rendition offered by the Master the better so far as the audience is concerned. The lyrics are included here with the kind permission of the Company:

Oh! give us your plain dealing fellows,
Who never from honesty shrink,
Not thinking of all they shall tell us,
But telling us all that they think.

So give us your plain dealing fellows, etc.
Truth from man flows like wine from a bottle,
His free-spoken heart's a full cup;
But when truth sticks halfway in the throttle
Man's worse than a bottle cork'd up.

So give us your plain dealing fellows, etc.
Complaisance's a gingerbread creature,
Used for show, like a watch, by each spark,
But truth is a golden repeater
Which sets a man right in the dark.

So give us your plain dealing fellows, etc.
Half-words, shrugs and nods – a deceiver –
The cunning man's art to seem wise,
But, trust me, plain-dealers will ever
Such paltry practice despise.
So give us your plain dealing fellows, etc.

The Worshipful Company of Carmen

The Carmen's Company has its own hymn sung to the tune *Wareham* (more commonly sung to the words *Rejoice, O land, in God Thy Might*). The hymn is sung at its annual Foundation Day Service, kindly included here by permission of the Company:

O God of virtue, might and fame
Fulfil in us our humble aim
To be possessed of steadfast skill,
Yet swift and sure to do thy will.

How glad we see thy foes defied
By Katharine, our saintly guide,
Who so bestirs this ancient guild,
Our faith with new resolve we build!

Upon the wheel of her distress
Did she thy noble cause confess,
And when her soul to thee had soared,
A glorious crown was her reward.

Grant, Lord, like her, that we may win;
Cleanse thou our hearts from shame and sin;
And let us ever strive to heed
The cries of those in direst need!

Most gracious Father, now we pray,
Preserve us in the middle way,
And lead us past each fearsome bend
To gates flung wide at journey's end.

The Worshipful Company of Distillers

In 2019, the Clerk to the Distillers' Company was encouraged to write a song for the Company. It was first performed at the Company's February luncheon in 2020, which turned out to be the Company's last formal event prior to the national lockdown enforced by the COVID-19 pandemic. The song is titled *Good Heart* and at the time of writing the music was still being scored. The lyrics are included here by kind permission of the Company:

Chorus

'Twas from the Apothecaries that Sir Theodore broke free,
procuring a Charter from His late Majesty.
The Distillers of London thus came to be born,
a new Guild in the City, heralding a new dawn.

Those distilling strong waters in London and beyond,
were suddenly subjected to us under bond.
For the Company of Distillers was empowered by the Crown,
to inspect, and to fine, with the right to close down!

Chorus

But our friends in the City they had other ideas,
our Charter was not ratified for 30 long years.
With Civil War in England and the renaissance abroad,
it was perhaps not surprising our progress had stalled.

We continued to be sanguine – Droppe as Raine, Distill as Dewe –
and the Aldermen relented in 1672.
69 in the rankings, with a monopoly to boot,
it was surely inevitable we would get fat on the loot.

Chorus

The Indian and Russe on our arms as displayed,
gives clues to our links with the wealthy spice trade.
The world was our oyster, monopoly the game;
we had all the ingredients for riches and fame.

But King William of Orange and Hogarth's Gin Lane,
conspired to ensure things were never the same.
The infamous Gin Acts proved a complete wrecking ball: for
we never got rich; and never purchased a Hall!

Chorus

The 20th century saw changes galore,
a realignment with our industry like never before.
With new Corporate Freemen, the Gin Guild and more,
in the 21st century we have come to the fore.

So give thanks to the Master, the Wardens and Clerk(!),
for encouraging our Company to make its true mark!
From modest beginnings we have come a long way,
so here's to our future, our prosperity and sway.

Chorus

Good heart, ye Distillers, and let's raise a glass,
to our most ancient of liveries, our founder and craft.

The Worshipful Company of Drapers

In 1931, Past Master Dr Arthur E Giles published several of his verses in a book titled *A Fantasy of the Seasons*. In the foreword Dr Giles wrote: "In publishing this book of verse at the request of personal friends I am conscious that their partiality exaggerates the merit of what is submitted to them. Nevertheless, I hope that some of my verses may appeal also to unknown and therefore unbiased readers". Included in the book is the song of the Drapers Company:

When great King Edward's wise decree
Bestowed the Drapers' Charter,
He gave them leave, from trammels free
Their goods to sell and barter.

King Henry's charter placed the guild
In Holy Mary's keeping,
To show that men should worship yield
Nor live alone for cheaping.

Our Fellowship enjoineth love
As that which most availeth;
For work and worship fruitless prove
When loving kindness faileth.

Chorus

While such traditions hold their sway
The hope we still shall nourish
That, root and branch, the Drapers may
For ever live and flourish.

The Worshipful Company of Farmers

Although not a Company song as such, the Farmers' Company is known to sing that old English country ballad, *The Farmer's Boy*, at formal banquets. This song is also the regimental quick march of the Princess of Wales's Royal Regiment.

The Worshipful Company of Fletchers

The Company has five songs, four of which were created in 1818 and a fifth in 1820, all by Samuel Arnott (a member of the Company). The first four songs were composed to be played at the Company's four court meetings in 1818 and were presented to the Father of the Company.

The lyrics to the fifth of the Company's songs are included here with kind permission of the Company. It is sung to the tune of *Roast Beef of Old England*:

> *Once more with great pleasure, each brother we meet,*
> *In friendship and harmony share a gay treat,*
> *May no sad reverse the good Fletchers defeat;*
> *And sing oh the gay days of the Fletchers,*
> *And sing oh the good Fletchers gay days.*
>
> *To the King and the Fletchers a bumper display,*
> *May great commerce and liberty make Britons gay,*
> *May our happy charters ne'er come to day;*
> *And sing oh the gay days of the Fletchers,*
> *And sing oh the good Fletchers gay days.*
>
> *To our worthy Wardens respect let us pay,*
> *With thanks for their care of us on each past day,*
> *With them Fletchers comfort will never decay;*
> *And sing oh the gay days of the Fletchers,*
> *And sing oh the good Fletchers gay days.*
>
> *To each absent brother with pleasure we will,*
> *Each prospect in life may they live to fulfil,*
> *With kind live and friendship each full moment kill;*
> *And sing oh the gay days of the Fletchers,*
> *And sing oh the good Fletchers gay days.*

To the Fletchers good laisse let's fill ere we part,
From the true paths of wedlock may they never depart,
From fond joys domestic may Fletchers ne'er start;
And sing oh the gay days of the Fletchers,
And sing oh the good Fletchers gay days.

In peace and calm joy may we finish the year,
No sad state commotion may Old England fear,
To freedom with loyalty happily steer.
And sing oh the roast beef of Old England,
And sing of the Old English roast beef.

The Fletchers' Company also has a hymn which dates from at least 1545, from *Toxophilus* by Roger Ascham, a 16th- century scholar who was a tutor to Elizabeth I and dedicated his work on the love of archery to Henry VIII.

And thus I pray God that al Fletchers getting their lyvynge
truly and al archers vsynge shootynge honestly,
and al manner of men that favour artillery,
may lyve continuallye in healthe and meriness,
obeying theyr prince as they shude
and loving God as they ought,
to whom for al things be al honour and glorye
for ever.
Amen.

The Worshipful Company of Grocers

First sung in 1845, the Grocers' Company song was written to commemorate the 500th anniversary of the Company's first Royal Charter. The song was largely forgotten until 2017 when it was discovered in the Company's archive. It was sung in May 2018 to celebrate the Mayoral year of Sir Charles Bowman, Citizen and Grocer. The song is sung to the tune of The Vicar of Bray. Here, courtesy of the Grocers' Company, is the chorus to its song:

> *Then send round the bowl*
> *Which enlivens the soul*
> *We've a subject that makes the heart glow, sir.*
> *Fill high to the toast*
> *That we all honour most*
> *The Church, The Queen and The Grocers!*

The Worshipful Company of Horners

Devotees of Messrs Flanders and Swann might be pleased to learn that since 1991 the Horners' Company made liberal use of the tune and some of the words from *A Song of Patriotic Prejudice* when creating its own Company song. There are three versions of the song, performances of which rotate annually. The first version, performed since 1991, was written by John Hann. A video of the song being performed by Past Master Emeritus Jeremy Cartwright may be viewed at: https://vimeo.com/418083529

> *Most Livery Comp'nies are terribly old;*
> *And some are quite dashing, and others quite bold.*
> *Some Comp'nies have vanished, but one's here to stay;*
> *It beats all the others – or so I've heard say.*
>
> *The Horners, the Horners, the Horners are best;*
> *I wouldn't give tuppence for all of the rest.*
>
> *The Plaisterer's Hall is extremely ornate;*
> *The Hall of the Grocers contains an iron gate.*
> *The Horners are diff'rent, we don't have a hall;*
> *So, darkly, we mutter, 'To hell with them all'.*

Except Painter Stainers, our friends, whom we greet,
'Cos their hall's the place where we all drink and eat.

The Blacksmiths, they hammer on iron and on steel;
They're brawny and muscular – never genteel.
The Horners have stamina, elan and zest;
And that's why there's no doubt that we are the best.

The Butchers are quaint, in their Liv'ry they mince;
The Fruiterers dress in a pale shade of quince.
The Weavers keep warm in a woolly string vest;
The· Scriv'ners wear plumes but, then what of the rest?

In order of precedence, Mercers come first;
The Brewers are fourteenth in spite of their thirst.
The Grocers and Drapers come second and third;
But we think this ranking supremely absurd.
So, down with the Great Twelve, and down with the rest;
The Horners, though fifty-fourth, are clearly the best.

The Goldsmiths have gold, and the Brewers have beer;
The latter is cheap, and the former is dear.
The Cutlers have knives, and the dyers have dye.
But we have our horn – so here's mud in your eye.

We have to admit that the Masons can build.
Like Tylers and Bricklayers, they have their Guild.
The Joiners and Ceilers are clumsy, and slow;
And Vintners are boozy – and hawkish you know;
They'll get their swan-uppance along with the rest;
So three cheers for us, 'cos the Horner's are best.

So raise up your glasses good Horners I pray;
A toast to the Master on this special day.
Hooray for our Wardens, our Beadle and Clerk;
Three cheers for our guests this have been quite a lark.

The Horners, the Horners, the Horners are best;
I wouldn't give tuppence for all of the rest.

The other two versions were written by Dr Denis Cruse. The second version is as follows:

110 Livery Companies there are
Some older, some younger, among them a star
The Horners, though middling in precedence be
We outshine all others in every degree

The Horners, the Horners, the Horners are best
I wouldn't give tuppence for all of the rest!

No Needlemaker can see eye-to-eye
With shoddy Clothmakers whose produce they spy,
And Butchers' meat rots and then maggots grow fat,
While our horn and plastics don't go off like that

The Farmers and Gardeners are muddy and cold
The Woolmen should all stay at home in their fold
The Bowyers and Fletchers their best-by dates passed
But Horners have stamina – boy do we last!

At mention of Loriners we bridle a lot
And as for Gunmakers – of them we're well shot
The Wheelwrights and Turners we roundly abuse
Glass Sellers are pains and we see through their ruse

The Dyers still live but the Carmen don't sing
The Masons are blockheads, the Goldsmiths make bling.
Apothecaries fleece you for drugs they display,
While Barbers will operate – keep out of their way

The Skinners kill rabbits and creatures like these,

With Taylors swap places to keep City peace,
They used to be violent, they've both kept fine Halls,
At sixes and sevens they've now got no cause

We've Bankers, Insurers and Actuaries now,
These jonny-come-latelys won't really know how
Without years of history, tradition well-tried
To party and sing of their craft with our pride

For Painters and Stainers we've quite a fond heart,
They lend us their Hall with its impressive art
But Horners have bottle, all others allow
We know we're the tops so sing up with me now:

The Horners, the Horners, the Horners are best
I wouldn't give tuppence for all of the rest!

The third version, also by Dr Denis Cruse, is as follows:

110 Livery Companies there are
Some older, some younger, among them a star
The Horners, are top of the city somehow
The Mercers are history – we live for now,

The Horners, the Horners, the Horners are best
I wouldn't give tuppence for all of the rest!

Fishmongers and Butchers have uses, we'd say
But their products spoil after barely one day,
While our horn and plastics are lasting and used
In industry, lighting and packaging food

The Carpenters' wit is just wooden and plane,
But the Cutlers is sharp and their jibes give you pain
The Comp'ny of Fletchers can well make their point
While the Joiners are wilder – they'll roll you a joint

We don't understand what makes Clockmakers tick
The Tallow and Wax Chandlers get on our wick,
The Glovers have fingers in too many pies,
And the Bakers have trouble in making things rise

The Mercers and Grocers – shopkeepers are they,
The Fanmakers blow, hot and cold through the day
Wolf whistles at girls is the Bricklayers' trick,
And Plaisterers' boasting is laid on too thick

Distillers and Vintners now they might be missed,
I've heard at their banquets they all must desist
From throwing the empties at Lord Mayors and such,
Innkeepers and Brewers aren't better by much

Now Fuellers, Art Scholars and Marketors bow
To elders and betters who really know how,
With history behind them and pageantry tried
To celebrate craft that they sing of with pride

For Painters and Stainers we've quite a fond heart,
They lend us their Hall with its impressive art
But Horners have bottle, all others allow
We know we're the tops so sing up with me now,

The Horners, the Horners, the Horners are best
I wouldn't give tuppence for all of the rest!

The Worshipful Company of Joiners and Ceilers

The Jolly Joiners (as their Twitter account attests) has two songs; the first is that of the Joiners which is usually sung to the tune of *The Vicar of Bray*. The second is Heart of Oak, the March of the Royal Navy. The lyrics are included here with the kind permission of the Company:

The Joiners

'Twas good Queen Bess our Charter gave
To Joiners skilled and wise
And though four hundred years have passed
Their deeds we'll not despise

Though years have passed and sped away,
But still our tree has root,
New branches grafted on its stem
Bring forth more glorious fruit

Let Brother Joiner hand in hand
Their friendship never sever
But drink the toast "Our Brotherhood"
And may it last for ever

We strive with others to keep pace
And have not been behind
The student in our Joiners Craft
A helping hand will find
And those admitted to our ranks
Will ne'er regret the day,
But the heart and voice join in the toast
Our Master gives, and say –

Let Brother Joiner hand in hand
Their friendship never sever
But drink the toast "Our Brotherhood"
And may it last for ever

Heart Of Oak

Come cheer up, my lads! 'tis to glory we steer,
To add something more to this wonderful year;

133

To honour we call you, not press you like slaves,
For who are so free as the sons of the waves?

Chorus
Heart of oak are our ships, heart of oak are our men;
We always are ready, steady, boys, steady!
We'll fight and we'll conquer again and again.

We ne'er see our foes but we wish them to stay,
They never see us but they wish us away;
If they run, why we follow, and run them ashore,
For if they won't fight us, we cannot do more.

Chorus

They swear they'll invade us, these terrible foes,
They frighten our women, our children, and beaus;
But should their flat bottoms in darkness get o'er,
Still Britons they'll find to receive them on shore.

Chorus

Still Britain shall triumph, her ships plough the sea,
Her standard be justice, her watchword "Be free";
Then cheer up, my lads! with one heart let us sing:
Our soldiers, our sailors, our statesmen and King.

Chorus

The verses were written by the actor/manager David Garrick in 1759 to
celebrate Hawke's victory at Quiberon Bay. Set to music by "Past
Master" William Boyce for a "Christmas Pantomime " called Harlequins
Invasion at the Theatre Royal, Dury Lane. The rhythm is said to be that

of the beat of "action stations" calling all hands to quarters and the ship prepared for action.

The Worshipful Company of Marketors

Tasoulla Christou, wife of Past Master Richard Christou, has written a number of pieces that have been performed atMarketors' Company events. In 2018, she dedicated an anthem (Psalm 150: *Praise Ye the Lord*) to this modern Livery Company. A recording of the anthem may be found on YouTube.

The Mercers' School Song

The Company had a school which closed in 1959. While not strictly a Livery Company song, the lyrics of the *Mercers' School Song* are reproduced here with the kind permission of the Company:

> *Carmen Mercerense*
>
> *Fundatorum pietatem decet celebrare*
> *Misterae Communitatem Mercerae laudare*
> *Gratis animis laudemus*
> *Magna voce celebremus*
> *Neve canere cessmus*
> > *Honor Deo!*
>
> *Quondam hospites nos aedis sacrae Aconensis*
> *Hospiti nunc tenet sedes prisca Barnardensis*
> *Novu praecepti heredes –*
> *Ecce supra focos vides! –*
> *Regi atque regno fides.*
> > *Honor Deo!*

135

Fidem principi praestemus: Deum honorare,
Necnon memores debemus Deo grates dare:
Tria ex avis accepta
Nec discipulis inepta
Usque servemus praecepta,
Honor Deo!

Sexto Henrico Beato auspice fundatae
Felici plus quinque fato saecula servatae
Scholae splendidam historiam
Sine maculis memoriam
Integram tradamus gloriam:
Honor Deo!

The Worshipful Company of Parish Clerks

In 2000, the Worshipful Company of Parish Clerks heard the debut performance of the Company's *Millennium Anthem* (set to the words of Psalm 98).

The Company also has a song which is sung at every dinner:

CARMEN CLERICORUM

Now to heaven our thoughts we raise,   *Elevate mentem.*
Sind we loud our song of praise,   *Ad Omnipotentem.*
Voice and organ now conspire,   *Deum, te laudamus.*
Priest and people, clerk and choir,   *Laete gaudeamus.*

Praise him for our Company,   *Digne venerato.*
Happy may our Master be,   *Salve coronatus.*
Now for every Clerk we pray,   *Nominis honesti.*
In this City here today,   *Celebremus festi.*

Glory to the Father sing,   *Deo Civitatus.*

To the Son our praises bring,	*Dato pro peccatis.*
Holy Ghost thy blessings pour,	*Tibi sit victoria.*
Trinity, for evermore,	*In excelsis gloria.*

Carmen Clericorum was the final event of the masque first performed in 1972, with text by Canon Richard Tydeman, former Rector of St Sepulchre-without-Newgate and a former member of the Company, who proved his skill as a storyteller, a versifier and Latiniser, as the*Carmen* illustrates. The music is by Andrew Pearmain

The Worshipful Company of Security Professionals

The Security Professionals is a Modern Livery Company that boasts a theme for orchestra. It was commissioned by Stuart Seymour and written by Samuel Bordoli in 2015.

The Worshipful Company of Skinners

The Skinners' Company celebrates the election of its Master and four Wardens in an annual ceremony held in the Company's hall. While there is no single piece of music for the event, the Master's school, career, heritage and hobbies are usually reflected in a piece played by a brass quartet.

The outgoing Master toasts the Master Elect and the four Wardens in turn by drinking from a substantial golden cup in the shape of a cockerel. At the same time, each of the newly elected officers is crowned with a cap.

The accompanying music becomes progressively more distorted with each toast – perhaps reflecting the effect of the Master drinking five times from such a fulsome vessel!

The Worshipful Company of Tax Advisers

The Worshipful Company of Tax Advisers has its own song with lyrics by the Company's Clerk, Stephen Henderson. It is sung to the tune of Elgar's *Land of Hope and Glory*. The Company informs us that the song is usually sung with the accompaniment of napkin waving! The song's lyrics are included here by kind permission of the Company and the Clerk.

> *We're The Tax Advisers*
> *Modern Company,*
> *We advise everybody*
> *E'en The Mayoralty.*
> *No remuneration*
> *All for Charity,*
> *When your books are balanced*
> *We're in ecstasy (dah dah dah)*
> *All shall bow before us,*
> *Even HM (breath) RC.*

Note: The song is followed by cheering, applause, waving, etc.

The Worshipful Company of Tin Plate Workers alias Wire Workers

The Worshipful Company of Tin Plate Workers alias Wire Workers processes into dinner to the tune of *The Parade of the Tin Soldiers* by Léon Jessel.

The Worshipful Company of Turners

In a departure from the usual jolly nature of Livery Company songs, the Turners' Company boasts the *Ballad of Anne Warren*, who was publicly executed by burning in 1616. Anne was convicted of murdering her husband John, a man who was a well-respected Gentleman and Turner resident in Cow Lane near to Smithfield. At the time, murder of a husband by a wife would have been Petty Treason.

The Worshipful Company of Tylers and Bricklayers

The Tylers and Bricklayers' Company processes in to dinner with a march composed by Edward Nesbit.

The Worshipful Company of Vintners

The Vintners' Company song was written in 1702 for a pageant given in honour of Queen Anne. Nowadays, the song is sung at Company banquets and is followed by five cheers for the Master, recalling an event in the 14th century when the Master hosted five kings at dinner, several of whom were released from the Tower of London for the evening (they were held for ransom). The event is commemorated on a plaque in Vintners' Hall.

A recording of the Vintners' Company song may be listened to on the Company's website along with a copy of the words and musical score: https://vintners.company/the-company/vintners-song/

The Worshipful Company of Woolmen

The Worshipful Company of Woolmen processes in to dinner to the tune of Percy Grainger's *Shepherd's Hey*.

The Worshipful Company of World Traders

To celebrate the Company's 10th anniversary in 2010, a musical accompaniment to the Company's prayer was commissioned. It was first played in 2011 when a stained-glass window was unveiled in All-Hallows-by-the-Tower (the Company's church).

> *Commerce between the nations,*
> *Sharing the bounty God has given,*
> *May we work to develop opportunities for all.*
> *Friendship, nations, working closely with one another,*
> *May we seek to encourage Harmony between us all.*
> *Commerce and honest friendship;*
> *The bonds of trade draw us together,*
> *May we strive to work harder.*
> *Improving the world for us all.*
> *We dedicate a window to mark our first decade.*
> *May we celebrate our efforts,*
> *To promote trade with all,*
> *Commerce and honest friendship;*
> *The bonds of trade draw us together,*
> *May we strive to work harder,*
> *Improving the world for us all.*

Sung graces

Many of the City's Livery Companies share the sung grace, taken from *Laudi Spirituali* of 1545 (with a 19th-century harmonisation). It is also used by Masonic Lodges.

Laudi Spirituali

> *For these and all Thy mercies given.*
> *We bless and praise Thy name, O Lord,*
> *May we receive them with thanksgiving, Ever trusting in Thy Word,*
> *To Thee alone be honour, glory,*
> *Now and henceforth, for evermore, Amen.*

Salters' Company grace

The Worshipful Company of Salters is one of the Great Twelve Livery Companies of the City of London. The Company has its own grace, which is usually sung by former students of the Guildhall School of Music and Drama to the tune of The Old Hundredth Psalm from the *Genevan Psalter* (1551). The lyrics of the grace are included here with the kind permission of the Company:

> *Ye are the salt of the earth;*
> *Let your light so shine before men,*
> *that they may see your good works,*
> *and glorify your Father which is in heaven,*
> *and glorify your Father which is in heaven,*
>
> *Praise God, from whom all blessings flow;*
> *Praise him, all creatures here below,*

Praise him above ye heavenly host;
Praise Father, Son and Holy Ghost.
Amen.

Musicians' Company grace: *Oculi Omnium*

Charles Wood, composer and latterly Cambridge Professor of Music, wrote two musical settings of verses taken from Psalm 145: *The Eyes of All Wait Upon Thee, O Lord*. One of these settings was the winning entry in a prize competition in 1904 of the Worshipful Company of Musicians to compose a sung grace setting. This setting is still frequently used before Company banquets, often sung by choir members of St Paul's Cathedral.

Other pieces of music with City connections

The following pieces have a connection with the City of London, its institutions or closely affiliated regiments:

- *A Linden Antiphon*, composed by Alex Woolf, text by Paul Munden, commissioned in 2021 for a short film, *City Founded on Music*

- *Heare us, heare us, Lord* by Michael Berkeley CBE (Baron Berkeley of Knighton), commissioned in 2017 by the Worshipful Company of Apothecaries

- *Deus, portus pacis* by Cecilia McDowall, commissioned in 2009 for St Cecilia's Day at St Paul's Cathedral

- *Hodie! A Christmas Carmen* by John Roper, commissioned in 2014 by Geoffrey Purves while Master of the Worshipful Company of Architects

- *City Scenes* by Tasoulla Christou (Liveryman Musician and wife of the Master Marketor 2018–2019)

- *The Song of the Building*, composed by Donald Swann for the 850th anniversary of St Bartholomew's Hospital and the Priory Church of St Bartholomew the Great in 1973

- *Fanfare for the Lord Mayor of London*, composed by Sir Arthur Bliss (Master of the Queen's Music) in 1968

- *National Anthem* (first sung in Merchant Taylors' Hall)

- *A Song for the Lord Mayor's Table*, a cycle of six songs for soprano and piano forte by Sir William Walton (1902) based on poems by Blake, Wordsworth and others.

- *The Lord Mayor's Coachman*

  Of which there are two different songs:

  https://www.youtube.com/watch?v=aRg7mY9_TOQ

  http://monologues.co.uk/musichall/Songs-L/Lord-Mayors-Coachman.htm

- *To the City of London* by Ronald Corp (Liveryman of the Musicians' Company)

- *The British Grenadiers* – Quick March of the Honourable Artillery Company and the Royal Regiment of Fusiliers

- *The Duke of York* – Slow March of the Honourable Artillery Company

- *The British Grenadiers* – Quick March of the Royal Regiment of Fusiliers

- *Rule Britannia* – Slow March of the Royal Regiment of Fusiliers

- *Bonnie Dundee* – Canter of the Light Cavalry HAC

- *The Keel Row* – Trot of the Light Cavalry HAC

- *The Duchess of Kent* – Walk of the Light Cavalry HAC

- *The Lord Mayor* – Part catch, part glee by James Green (1790)

Reproduced here by kind permission of Ashworth Informatics – Ray Hall for the Aldrich Catch Club:

The Lord Mayor, the aldermen and common council too, the turtle-eating citizens, in all a jovial crew.

There was a weak man, a strong man, a short man and a long man, a lean man, a fat man, a tall man, a squat man, the turtle-eating citizens, in all a jovial crew.

They put the bottle round and filled up every glass, and he who has no wife to drink may drink his fav'rite lass: the turtle-eating citizens, in all a jovial crew.

Then after they had drank about, they cram sweetmeats and jellies, they never flinch, no not an inch, until they've filled their bellies, the turtle-eating citizens, in all a jovial crew.

In 1937, the composer Sir William Walton set to music the poem *In Honour of the City of London* by the Scottish Poet William Dunbar (1459–1530). Walton's composition is for a full orchestra and eight-part choir. The composition was performed in February 1992 by the Philharmonia and The Bach Choir in the Royal Festival Hall. The Lord Mayor, Sir Brian Jenkins, was in attendance. A recording of the performance is available on YouTube.

> *London, thou art of townes a per se.*
> *Soveraign of cities, seemliest in sight,*
> *Of high renoun, riches and royaltie;*
> *Of lordis, barons, and many a goodly knyght;*
> *Of most delectable lusty ladies bright;*
> *Of famous prelatis, in habitis clericall;*
> *Of merchauntis full of substaunce and of myght:*
> *London, thou art the flour of Cities all.*

> *Gladdith anon, thou lusty Troynovaunt,*
> *Citie that some tyme cleped was New Troy;*
> *In all the erth, imperiall as thou stant,*
> *Pryncesse of townes, of pleasure and of joy,*
> *A richer restith under no Christen roy;*
> *For manly power, with craftis naturall,*
> *Fourmeth none fairer sith the flode of Noy:*
> *London, thou art the flour of Cities all.*

> *Gemme of all joy, jasper of jocunditie,*
> *Most myghty carbuncle of vertue and valour;*
> *Strong Troy in vigour and in strenuytie;*
> *Of royall cities rose and geraflour;*
> *Empress of townes, exalt in honour;*
> *In beawtie beryng the crone imperiall;*
> *Swete paradise precelling in pleasure;*
> *London, thou art the flour of Cities all.*

> *Above all ryvers thy Ryver hath renowne,*

Whose beryall stremys, pleasaunt and preclare,
Under thy lusty wallys renneth down,
Where many a swan doth swymme with wyngis fair;
Where many a barge doth saile and row with are;
Where many a ship doth rest with top-royall.
O, towne of townes! patrone and not compare,
London, thou art the flour of Cities all.

Upon thy lusty Brigge of pylers white
Been merchauntis full royall to behold;
Upon thy stretis goeth many a semely knyght
In velvet gownes and in cheynes of gold.
By Julyus Cesar thy Tour founded of old
May be the hous of Mars victoryall,
Whose artillary with tonge may not be told:
London, thou art the flour of Cities all.

Strong be thy wallis that about thee standis;
Wise be the people that within thee dwellis;
Fresh is thy ryver with his lusty strandis;
Blith be thy chirches, wele sownyng be thy bellis;
Rich be thy merchauntis in substaunce that excellis;
Fair be their wives, right lovesom, white and small;
Clere be thy virgyns, lusty under kellis:
London, thou art the flour of Cities all.

Thy famous Maire, by pryncely governaunce,
With sword of Justice thee ruleth prudently.
No Lord of Parys, Venyce, or Floraunce
In dignitye or honour goeth to hym nigh.
He is exampler, loode-ster, and guye;
Principall patrone and rose orygynalle,
Above all Maires as maister most worthy:
London, thou art the flour of Cities all.

In 2020, Alderman Sir Andrew Parmley wrote new lyrics for the Major General's Song from The Pirates of Penzance based on the Order of Precedence.

The origins of Liv'ry in the City are a "mystery";
The reason for the numbering is lost in mists of history;
It was in 1515 when the precedence was ratified;
Since when the Great Twelve Companies have always seemed quite satisfied.
The Mercers sit at number one, the Grocers are at number two;
Then Drapers, Fish and Goldsmiths come, with Skinners and the MTs, who
Not wanting to be number seven, assert they should be number six,
A paradox the Lord Mayor sorted with a simple City fix:
To be at sixes and at sevens is an English paradox,
To be at sixes and at sevens is an English paradox,
To be at sixes and at sevens is an English paradox.
The Haberdashers, Salters and the Ironmongers follow next;
The Vintners and the Clothworkers and Dyers – thirteen – always vexed;
In short in matters civic and in language mathematical
The Weavers are the hardest hit by order categorical.
The Brewers, Leathersellers and the Pewterers are next in line;
Then Barbers, Cutlers, Bakers and Wax Chandlers in their liv'ry fine;
Then Tallow Chandlers, Armourers and Girdlers and the Butchers trot;
With Saddlers, Carpenters and Cordwainers – oh! what a funny lot!
The Company of Painters and the Curriers established next
Then Masons, Plumbers, Innholders and Founders found the ancient text

To welcome Poulters, Cooks and Coopers, Tylers and the Brick
Layers too;
And male-only[4] Bowyers Master who uniquely serves for two.
(Years, that is.)
A two-year term for Bowyers – it's a job that only men dare
do,
A two-year term for Bowyers – it's a job that only men dare
do,
A two-year term for Bowyers – it's a job that only men dare
men dare do.
The Fletchers and the Blacksmiths and the Joiners are the next
in line;
Then come ourselves at 42, some say the finest of the fine;
In short in matters civic and in language mathematical
The Weavers are the hardest hit by order categorical.
There follow many more – some ancient and a few
contempor'ry
The modern ones include the Cleaners and the jolly Actu'ry;
The Educators and the Art Scholars are new kids on the block;
The ITs and the Firemen and the Woolmen with their City
flock;
The Horners are a happy lot, the Framework Knitters know
what's knot;
The Mariners are "hon'rable", the Gardeners tend their little
plot;
Distillers know their armagnac, their gin and scotch and
vodka too;
Musicians like a tipple and, believe me, they can sink a few!
The Weavers are the oldest and they should be known as
number one,
The Weavers are the oldest and they should be known as
number one,

---

[4] The Bowyers' Company has since removed this restriction.

The Weavers are the oldest and they should be known as number number one.

The Liv'ry is an ancient lot of Masters quite adventury;

And Weavers know that they've been number one across the centuries;
In short in matters civic and in language mathematical
The Weavers should be number one in order categorical.

A video of the song being performed by Liveryman Tony Saunders may be viewed here: https://youtu.be/CMOR7_Hi12U

Bibliography

The following is a selected bibliography of books on musical subjects associated with the City of London:

Apollo's Swan and Lyre (History of the Worshipful Company of Musicians, by Richard Crewdson)

Visitor's Guide to the City Churches (Tucker, 2013)

Temple Church, Revd Canon Joseph Robinson, Jarrold Publishing 1997, reprinted 2008.

Middle Temple – A Guide, The Honourable Society of the Middle Temple, 2008.

Music, Musicians and Organs of St Michael's Cornhill, Jonathan Rennert, Embassy Press Ltd, London, 2010.

A History of the St Michael's Singers, Harold Darke, 1948.

St Michael's Cornhill, Peter Hughes, 2007.

The Organs of the City of London from the Restoration to the Present, Nicholas M. Plumley, Positif Press, Oxford, 1996.

The English Chorister – A History, Alan Mould, Continuum Books, 2007.

Faith in the City of London, Niki Gorick, Unicorn Publishing, 2020.

Gresham College lecture: *The History and Music of the Spanish and Portuguese Jewish Congregation in the City of London*, Bevis Marks Synagogue, 2011.

The National Pipe Organ Register, npor.org.uk, a service provided by the British Institute of Organ Studies.

Papers published by the Guildhall Historical Association

The City Waits, Alan Lamboll (1963)
Sounds that Hurt Not, Alderman Sir Gilbert Inglefield (1971)
Music in the City, Deputy Wilfred Dewhurst (1980)
Apollo's Swan and Lyre, Alderman Sir Andrew Parmley (2006)

Lord Mayors who have served as Master of the Musicians' Company

The following Aldermen have served in the offices of both Lord Mayor of the City of London, and Master of the Worshipful Company of Musicians:

Sir Andrew Parmley (2016) (see Foreword)
Sir Roger Gifford (2012)
Sir Alan Traill (1984)
Sir Gilbert Inglefield (1967)
Sir Denis Truscott (1957)
Sir Edward Ernest Cooper, Bt (1919)
Sir George Wyatt Truscott (1908)
Sir Brook Watson, Bt (1796)
Brass Crosby MP (1770)

For more details, see the Worshipful Company of Musicians' Archive website at https://www.wcomarchive.org.uk/--lord-mayors.

Locations of City churches

Most of the City's churches act as venues for concerts, choirs or other musical groups and performances. The locations of the churches in the City of London are as follows:

All Hallows by the Tower – Byward Street, London EC3R 5BJ
All Hallows on the Wall – London Wall, EC2M 5ND
Dutch Church – 7 Austin Friars, EC2N 2HA
St Alban the Martyr – Brooke Street, EC1N 7RD
St Andrew Holborn – 5 St Andrew Street EC4A 3AB
St Andrew Undershaft – St Mary Axe EC3A 8BN
St Andrew-by-the-Wardrobe – Queen Victoria Street, EC4V 5DE
St Anne and St Agnes – Gresham Street EC2V 7BX
St Bartholomew the Great – Cloth Fair, West Smithfield, EC1A 7JQ
St Bartholomew the Less – West Smithfield EC1A 7BE
St Benet – the Metropolitan Welsh Church – Queen Victoria Street EC4V 4ER
St Botolph Aldersgate – Aldersgate Street, EC1A 4EU
St Botolph Aldgate – Aldgate High Street EC3N 1AB
St Botolph Bishopsgate – Bishopsgate, EC2M 3TL
St Bride – Fleet Street, EC4Y 8AU
St Clement Eastcheap – Clements Lane, EC4N 7HB
St Dunstan in the West – 186a Fleet Street, EC4A 2HR
St Edmund, King and Martyr – Lombard Street, EC3V 9AN
St Giles Cripplegate – Fore Street, Cripplegate, EC2Y 8DA
St Helen's Bishopsgate – Great St Helen's EC3A 6AT
St James Garlickhythe – Garlick Hill EC4V 2AL
St Katharine Cree Church – 86 Leadenhall Street, EC3A 3BP
St Lawrence Jewry – Gresham Street, EC2V 5AA
St Magnus the Martyr – Lower Thames Street, EC3R 6DN
St Margaret Lothbury – Lothbury, EC2R 7HH
St Margaret Pattens – Rood Lane, EC3M 1HS
St Martin Ludgate – Ludgate Hill, EC4M 7DE
St Mary Abchurch – Abchurch Lane, EC4N 7BA

St Mary Aldermary – Watling Street, EC4M 9BW
St Mary-at-Hill – Lovat Lane, Eastcheap EC3R 8EE
St Mary Moorfields – 4–5 Eldon Street, EC2M 7LS
St Mary Woolnoth – Lombard Street, EC3V 9AN
St Mary-le-Bow – Cheapside EC2V 6AU
St Michael Cornhill – Cornhill EC3V 9DS
St Olave Hart Street – 8 Hart Street EC3R 7NB
St Peter upon Cornhill – Cornhill EC3V 3PD

Commercial suppliers

The following list of commercial suppliers may be of interest to readers. Inclusion in this list does not imply recommendation or endorsement. This list is included only for convenience and was kindly provided by the Livery Committee:

Edward Dye	http://www.edward-dye.com/
Elysium Brass	http://www.elysiumbrass.co.uk
Erika Gundesen	http://www.erikagundesen.co.uk
Felici Opera	http://www.feliciopera.com
Julian Cable	http://www.thecityminstrel.co.uk
Olivia Grace Piper	http://www.oliviagracepiper.com/
Olivia Jageurs	http://www.olivia-harpist.com/
World Heart Beat Academy	http://www.worldheartbeat.org/

About the authors

Paul Jagger is a Court Assistant of the Worshipful Company of Information Technologists. He is the author of The City of London Freeman's Guide (privately published) and City of London: Secrets of the Square Mile (published by Pavilion Books under the PITKIN imprint). In 2016, he received the City Livery Club's Root & Branch Award from the Lord Mayor of London. He is also a popular lecturer specialising in the City of London and its Livery Companies, their treasures and heraldry.

You may follow Paul on Twitter @CityandLivery

Julian Cable is a Liveryman of the Worshipful Company of Musicians. He holds an Honours Degree in Music from the University of Cambridge (Selwyn College), where he gained two Firsts, and an Associateship Diploma from the Royal College of Organists. While still at school, he gained a piano Performers' Diploma from the London College of Music, and also studied harmony and composition privately at the Royal Academy of Music. Julian performs regularly in concerts in London and elsewhere. He is also a choral singer (including with the Collegiate Singers at Westminster Abbey), organist, and composer.

You may follow Julian on Twitter @TheCityMinstrel

The City of London Freeman's Guide

Also available online in hardback and eBook format, The City of London Freeman's Guide is the definitive concise guide to the City of London's customs, ceremonies, traditions, institutions, officers and landmarks.